JOHN ROBERT COLOMBO

W9-CCD-646

The Midnight Hour

Canadian Accounts of Eerie Experiences

A HOUNSLOW BOOK
A MEMBER OF THE DUNDURN GROUP
TORONTO

Editorial Director: Anthony Hawke
Copy-Editor: Jennifer Bergeron
Design: Jennifer Scott
Printer: Friesens

National Library of Canada Cataloguing in Publication Data

The midnight hour : Canadian accounts of eerie experiences / John Robert Colombo, editor.

ISBN 1-55002-496-5

1. Supernatural. 2. Parapsychology — Canada. I. Colombo, John Robert, 1936–

BF1028.5.C3M44 2004   001.94'0971   C2003-907195-2

1   2   3   4   5   08   07   06   05   04

Conseil des Arts du Canada
Canada Council for the Arts
Canada
ONTARIO ARTS COUNCIL
CONSEIL DES ARTS DE L'ONTARIO

We acknowledge the support of the **Canada Council for the Arts** and the **Ontario Arts Council** for our publishing program. We also acknowledge the financial support of the **Government of Canada** through the **Book Publishing Industry Development Program** and **The Association for the Export of Canadian Books,** and the **Government of Ontario** through the **Ontario Book Publishers Tax Credit** program, and the **Ontario Media Development Corporation's Ontario Book Initiative.**

Dundurn Press
8 Market Street
Suite 200
Toronto, Ontario, Canada
M5E 1M6

Gazelle Book Services Limited
White Cross Mills
Hightown, Lancaster, England
LA1 4X5

Dundurn Press
2250 Military Road
Tonawanda NY
U.S.A. 14150

Thank

Marcello Truzzi

You

CONTENTS

PREFACE • 9

ACKNOWLEDGEMENTS • 17

NEWSPAPER ACCOUNTS • 19
A Wild Man / *The Morning Herald and Daily Advertiser* • 20
The Baldoon Mystery / *The Globe* • 25
The Gypsy Woman and the Lizards / *The Constitutional* • 32
Have Clothes Ghosts? / *The Evening News* • 36
Chinese Superstition / *The Cariboo Sentinel* • 39
Strange Tale of Horrors / *The Globe* • 41
Clairvoyant Physician / *The New Brunswick Reporter* • 45
A Haunted House / *Victoria Daily Colonist* • 49
B.C. Cannibals / *The Free Press* • 54
Remarkable Dreams / Reported by David Boyle in *The Globe* • 58
My Fight for Life with an Octopus /
Captain S.F. Scott & Lillan Ferguson in *The Daily News* • 61
The Weird Creature / *The Herald* • 67
Ugly Idol / *The Leader-Post* • 70
Premonition of Death / *Lethbridge Herald* • 73
"Caddy" the Sea Serpent / *The Dawson News* • 77
Curse of the Devil Woman / Roy Cooper in
The Winnipeg Free Press • 80

PERSONAL ACCOUNTS • 83

The Ghost of Mary Mowat / David Sztybel • 84

A House Near Peggy's Cove / "Richard" • 87

A Haunted House in Prescott / James F. Robinson • 89

La Vieille Chapelle Ramsay / John Robert Colombo • 92

The Haunted Duplex / "Lizard" • 95

No One Wanted to Sleep in the Room / Ron Sandler • 98

I Hope You Enjoyed These / "Michael" • 100

A Very Strange Experience / Kelly Kirkland • 103

The Ways of the Hierarchy / Elsie Kelly • 106

Fergus in Good Spirits / Jack Kohane • 117

It Was an Amazing Experience / "Ekin" • 122

The P.E.I. Hauntings / David K. MacKinnon •124

The Haunting Experience / Robert Buckman • 129

It Leaves One Wondering / Karin Dearness • 133

A Haunted House in Rockwood / Angie Laurus • 135

The Spoon Begins to Bend! / Allan Slaight & David Ben• 139

The Haunted Guitar / Patrick Cross • 145

Here's the Scoop / Brad Garside • 148

Two Experiences That Can Be Called Paranormal / "Lee" • 150

Actual Events / Susan George • 156

Everyone Found the Place Enchanting / Charlotte Fielden Morris • 161

Astral Travelling / Charlotte Fielden Morris • 163

About a House in Barrie / Chrysta Rowland • 166

Wrapped in a 'Bow / Thomas R. Birmingham • 173

The Canadian Nostradamus / John Robert Colombo • 178

The Art of Cold Reading / James Randi • 182

The Lady with the Lamp / Alexander (Sandy) Thornton-Trump • 187

Ghost Stories / Rodney Coreau • 193

The Ghost in the Health Club / Health Club Member • 196

The Dream Visit / Helen Hughes • 201

Instances of Prescience / Helen Hughes • 204

Roy's Story / Anita Welsh • 207

The Houses on Bishop Street / Lianne Gore • 217

Goosebumps / Sheila Greenberg • 225

A Most Spectacular Sight / Lucie Romanycia • 227

PREFACE

What about you?

Here are some questions for you, the reader, to consider.

- Do you believe in ghosts?
- Have you ever felt the presence of a spirit, or sensed an entity or a form of energy sweep past you?
- When was the last time you thought about a person and that person, out of the blue, phoned you?
- Have you ever sensed you were "taking dictation"?
- Could you describe what you saw in the sky as a UFO?
- Did you ever enter a house that people said was haunted — and unexpectedly feel a shiver of fear?
- Has a respected friend ever confided in you the details of an incredible or impossible experience?
- Was there a fortune-teller who told you things about yourself and your past that nobody else knew?
- How often have you experienced a premonition and then had it "come true"?

Rhetorical questions

These are rhetorical questions, of course.

There is no way for you to answer them — except to yourself.

If you answered "yes" to any one of them, this is the book for you. It offers fifty accounts of incredible experiences that were reported by responsible people, Canadians all.

But if you answered "no" to any or all of these questions, this is the book for you, too. It is especially for you, because while reading it you will experience something novel — sensations, emotions, thoughts, and intuitions that you might never have entertained in the past.

This book offers you an admission ticket to the Big Top where you may take a reserved seat to witness a strange spectacle: a three-ring, circus-like atmosphere with wild and death-defying "acts" of strange and incredible events and experiences.

These accounts are true, not works of the imagination.

Belief or disbelief

You do not have to believe in the supernatural, the paranormal, or the mysterious to enjoy the accounts in this book. (Look at me. I neither believe in them nor disbelieve in them. I am interested in these things, curious about them, and inquisitive about the facts and factors that accompany them.)

These accounts are psychological facts, if not psychical ones. It was the psychologist Carl Rogers who said, "Every fact is friendly."

I have no doubt that sociologists and psychologists are able to explain away many of these experiences. It would take a psychiatrist or two to deal with a few of them. Philosophers and theologians, if asked, would have interpretations of their own to offer. Literary critics might want to "deconstruct" these narratives — or memorates, to use my own word for them. Readers, however, are encouraged to read them and regard them as adventures in human and perhaps extra-human dimensions.

I call them memorates

These accounts are stories, and good stories at that, but they are not stories in the sense of fictitious narratives. They are stories in the sense that they are dramatic recreations in words of events and experiences that actually took place.

The words are those of the witnesses themselves, and so I like to call such first-hand reports *memorates*. A memorate is a witness's private account of an incredible event or experience that is recalled "for the record." It is recited in a circle of people, usually friends, and is not meant to convince anyone of anything.

The word *memorate* is used by folklorists to refer to a personal narrative told as truth which may be believed or disbelieved.

Beyond belief

Some of the memorates in this book are *ghost* stories because they are about ghosts and spirits, sightings and hauntings. But all of them are *ghostly* stories in that they deal with a whole host of "ghostly" events: disappearances, alarming coincidences, strange undertakings, miraculous healings … you name it.

As I mentioned, in the main the words of the accounts are those of the witnesses themselves. But do not assume that because something eerie or ghostly has been experienced by the narrator he or she now believes in ghostly happenings. Indeed, most of the informants are as puzzled about the "reality" behind these bizarre episodes as are their listeners and readers.

It is generally forgotten that psychical research was one of the interests of the American psychologist and pragmatist William James. Indeed, he devoted two decades of his professional life to research into psychical matters, and even served as president of both the British Society for Psychical Research and the American Society for Psychical Research. He tested mediums, attended séances, and conducted experiments in telepathy. He studied what came to be called ESP (extrasensory perception) — clairvoyance, precognition, and psychokinesis.

Today he would have called himself a parapsychologist as well as a psychologist. But through it all — investigation, research, study, writing, lecturing, publishing — he remained a pragmatist and a person committed to rationalism and to the scientific method. After twenty years he retired from the field. He felt that the time had been well spent but (in a rhetorical flourish) he concluded that God had elected this field to be one area of creation and of human endeavour that would remain perpetually clouded in doubt.

Indeed, doubt is more common than belief.

As Louis Dudek, one of my favourite poets and aphorists, noted, sadly, "There is enlightenment in questions, but only barbarism in belief."

These matters are beyond belief.

Motives are mixed

I said that these matters are beyond belief, but are they beyond comprehension?

They are not beyond comprehension; people tell these stories, these tales, these experiences, these encounters, in order to share them with other people. They are told for a social purpose and they are told as truth.

Critics and skeptics will claim the stories are fantasies, falsehoods, fabrications, or frauds. If they are fantasies, the people telling them suffer delusions or hallucinations because such things simply do not happen. If they are falsehoods, the people telling them are misleading their listeners for reasons of their own; perhaps the story has been "building" and improving in the telling. If they are fabrications, they seem to follow a pattern because they are part fact and part fantasy, but the proportion of each is not known and the pattern is one of mystification. If they are frauds, they are pretty weak because they are being told for reasons that have nothing to do with influence, power, or money.

No doubt the stories improve in the telling. After awhile, that is all that is left for the reader or listener after the episode: the story. The story stands or falls on its ability to hold its audience. The stories in this collection hold their readers.

About the title

If the title of the book is familiar to you, you are probably (like the compiler) an older person. If you are a younger reader, you *might* wonder about it. When I last checked the Internet for the two words *midnight hour*, I found that there were 1.2 million references available through the Google search engine.

The references are a varied lot: a rock group, two songs, two movies, two novels, a radio program, a painting, a media production house, a Web design service, a novelty song, a nonsense verse, even a Christian prayer of absolution. I could go on!

The immediate inspiration for the title was the words from the chorus of a novelty song that was popular in English music halls in the mid-1930s. The song is called "With Her Head Tucked Underneath Her Arm," with words written by R.P. Weston and Bert Lee and music composed by Harris Weston. It was a favourite of Stanley Holloway in Britain; Rudy Vallee and the Connecticut Yankees — surprise! — performed it at London's Palladium and released a hit recording of the catchy tune and surprising words in the United States.

The chorus goes like this:

> With her head tucked underneath her arm,
> She walks the bloody Tower,
> With her head tucked underneath her arm,
> At the midnight hour.

The head is that of the beautiful Anne Boleyn, one of two wives beheaded at the behest of King Henry VIII, and it is the Tower of London that she roams. Music halls may be long gone, but "With Her Head" continues to haunt people, especially radio listeners around Halloween.

Despite the fact that the comic poet Edward Lear made good use of the words in his novelty verse "The Dong with a Luminous Nose" — "And those who watch at that midnight hour / From Hall or Terrace, or lofty Tower" — any reference to "the midnight hour" is principally one that is fraught with fear. High noon may be a time of reckoning, but the midnight hour is the time of darkness, of dread, of fright, of fear, and of terror. Strange things happen when the hands of the clock reach up to mark twelve. They symbolically surrender to "the chimes at midnight," to "the powers of darkness."

In the Bible, midnight stands for deliverance. The people of Israel were delivered from bondage in Egypt at midnight (Exodus 12). Christians associate "the midnight hour" with spiritual deliverance (Matthew 25:96). In popular culture, midnight is the temporal gateway for ghosts and devils that will run riot at the summit of the Brocken, the magic mountain in the Hartz Mountain Range of Germany, the original "Night on Bald Mountain," *Walpurgisnacht*, the Witches' Sabbath.

That is more than enough background!

About the contents

There are two parts to this book.

The first part consists of newspaper accounts of unusual experiences that occurred in the past. They come from the columns of daily or weekly newspapers, and they make interesting and charming reading today. Readers in the nineteenth century were more demanding of their newspapermen than readers are today. They wanted long and sturdy stories. The editors of these newspapers, being responsive without being very demanding of their craft, supplied them, writing new ones or reprinting ones from other papers. Many of these stories received wide distribution across the Dominion, as editor after editor reprinted them for their readers. In this section you will read about houses infested with spirits and gypsy cures that were known across the continent. The early twentieth century was not congenial to long reports of mysterious doings. It proved to be a material-minded century, with world wars, depressions, and burgeoning systems of mass communications. So there are fewer and fewer newspaper accounts of this type as we approach our own time.

In the second part of this book, which deals with personal accounts, the reports of unusual experiences are contemporary ones, for they come from correspondence that I have had with men and women who are willing to describe what had occurred to them. The majority of the accounts appear here for the first time, and they appear in the words of the experiencers themselves, not in the paraphrases of reporters or interpreters. Any editing done has been kept to a minimum. Indeed, the newspaper accounts in the first part of the book required rather more editing than did the original memoirs in the second part.

Why "the midnight hour"?

Incredible events and experiences may occur to ordinary people at any hour of the day. Yet some of the most incredible episodes seem to occur at dawn and at dusk, as we are waking from sleep in the morning and as we are falling asleep in the evening. Psychologists have a way of describing such twilight states: dawn experiences are *hynopompic*; dusk experiences are *hypnagogic*. In the mystery religions of Ancient Greece, which held sway for more than one thousand years, the guide was known as the *mystagog* or the *hypnopomp*. Scientists today recognize various depths of sleep and that distortions of perception, cognition, and emotion are characteristic of certain levels. Symbolically, at least, the deepest point of sleep is the midnight hour.

I see this book as a collection of fifty or so "midnight hours."

ACKNOWLEDGEMENTS

I burnt the midnight oil in the company of my researcher Alice Neal and my friend and librarian Philip Singer of the Toronto Public Library system. Two fellow researchers drew my attention to accounts that I would otherwise have missed: Dwight Whalen of Niagara Falls, Ontario, and W. Ritchie Benedict of Calgary, Alberta. I am grateful to David Skene-Melvin of Toronto, Ontario, and Ed Butts of Guelph, Ontario. I have benefitted from informative discussions with Cyril Greenland and David A. Gotlib, as well as with Eric McMillan and David Gower, knowledgeable "powers that be" behind Skeptics Canada / Ontario Skeptics. Most gracious and helpful have been Matthew James Didier and Jennifer Krutilla, a brother and a sister team who in October 1997 established The Ghosts & Hauntings Research Society. They sponsor various meetings and outings in addition to overseeing their website, one that is reasonable, entertaining, and invaluable: *http://www.torontoghosts.org/*.

Once again, Tony Hawke of Hounslow Press and Kirk Howard of The Dundurn Group have assisted me in my endeavour to bring Canadiana in its many varieties and variations to the attention of readers. Editors Barry Jowett and Jennifer Bergeron saved me from not a few errors; those that remain are my own!

The devotion of my wife, Ruth, remains a private mystery. The book itself is dedicated to the memory of Marcello Truzzi, sociologist, inquirer rather than seeker, a great man who is now a great spirit enshrined in the memory of those who knew and prized him.

NEWSPAPER ACCOUNTS

A WILD MAN

A wild man? From the Lake of the Woods area of Ontario near the Manitoba and Minnesota border? Not likely, you might say, but an account of just such a man is printed here in its entirety. It is only 109 words long. Would that it were longer!

"Extract from a Genuine Letter from Florence: dated September 13th, 1784," appeared anonymously in *The Morning Herald and Daily Advertiser* (London, England), January 3, 1785.

Following the "Extract" is some speculation about how they —the wild man and the news item — might have got where they were. And, appended to the appendage, I have added a summary of my own thoughts on the matter.

A Wild Man

(from *The Morning Herald and Daily Advertiser*)

There is lately arrived in France, from America, a wild man, who was caught in the woods, 200 miles back from the Lake of the Woods, by a party of Indians; they had seen him several times, but he was so swift of foot, that they could by no means got up with him; till one day, having the good fortune to find him asleep, they seized and bound him. He is near seven feet high, covered with hair, has but little appearance of understanding, and is remarkably sullen and untractable: when he was taken, half a bear was found lying by him, which he had but just killed.

The "Extract" was found for me by W. Ritchie Benedict of Calgary. Ritchie is the studious sort of person who loves to conduct research and, as well, to speculate on the context of the offbeat stories that are the subject of his researches. Both Ritchie and I knew that this news item about the "wild man" had appeared anonymously in the columns of *The London Times* in 1785. We both knew that it had subsequently been quoted in popular articles about strange creatures. Finally, both of us knew that the writers of these magazine articles lacked the date of the appearance of the news item in *The Times*. After much searching on microfilmed newspapers that are more than two hundred years old, Ritchie found the news item in the issue of January 4, 1785. Here is what he wrote in a letter dated May 4, 2003:

> I was able to go up to the University this afternoon to check things out. I wasn't really too hopeful, as that particular piece has been mentioned in several articles about Bigfoot, but none of them were even able to pin down the date beyond the year. When I put the reel on, I noticed that it was featured under a section headed simply London. *The London Times* had gone into business just four days earlier with the title: *The Universal Daily Register*. The first owner/editor was listed as a Mr. J. Walter, and at first I assumed that he might be the one who placed the piece in the paper, based on something he heard or knew.
>
> I noticed that there were a number of other British newspapers for the late 18th century, and I wondered if I could find anything else. After a bit of digging, incredibly, I found a *second* account. It reads word for word the same as the one in your letter, but this one appeared a day earlier on January 3rd, 1785, in *The Morning (London) Herald and Daily Advertiser*. Just as with the *London Times* bit, it is sandwiched in with other information, this time between something about political news or sailing times in Italy, and something else. The interesting part is that the

column with all three pieces is headed: "Extract of a Genuine Letter from Florence dated: September 13th, 1784."

Besides adding confirmation to the original account, this raises some very unusual questions. Marseilles, France, is not all that far from Florence. Presumably, the ship carrying the "wild man" would have docked there, and the news would have spread to Italy, where it found its way into a letter and then went to the London newspapers. If we assume it took at least two months to cross the Atlantic, the capture had to have occurred sometime in the spring or summer of 1784. It might have occurred as far back as 1783, but it is hard to imagine keeping and feeding something that could kill a bear for an entire winter. There are three newspapers that the University has that are of 1784 vintage, one from what was then Upper Canada, one from Halifax and the third from Quebec, I believe. I am fairly certain that there was nothing in any of the three, but then perhaps it never made the newspapers on this side of the Atlantic. It was extremely lucky it made the *London Times*. Had it been four days earlier, posterity would never have known about it.

Strange Magazine No. 5 in 1990 briefly alluded to the account and the year in their Monster issue, which is where I got wind of it and was able to pin down the exact date. I was struck by the similarity in certain details to the purported capture of a Bigfoot by Indians in the U.S. Midwest in 1839, which I wrote up in an article for *Fate*. It was based on an item in the *Ottawa General Advertiser* of September 6th, 1839. The description is very similar — eight feet high, covered with hair, with a sullen attitude and little understanding. In both instances, one wonders what happened to the creature after he arrived in "civilization" (i.e., New

Orleans and France). In this instance, it must have been shipped from Montreal or Halifax — most likely Montreal. The question is how did they transport the creature that far?

Perhaps, when he got to France, he ended up in the Bastille or at least a travelling zoo. There are reports in Canadian newspapers circa 1765 of the Beast of Gevaudan which some feel is a hyena that someone imported back then. I think I remember reading somewhere that some of the nobility had private zoos so this is probably where any unusual creature would end up. At any rate, I hope this helps. It seems kind of unlikely after 218 years that we will ever know much more about it.

What is interesting here is that Ritchie has given us a scenario that accounts for the provenance of the creature, its whereabouts in 1785, and its possible fate: incarceration in a private zoo. It is also of interest that the original news item (all 109 words of it) sparked Ritchie's lengthy speculation (all 655 words of it)! No doubt he is right when he says that we are unlikely to learn more than we know today about the nature of this "wild man."

Yet who knows? The incident may continue to spark the interest of people today, just as accounts of the Beast of Gévaudan continue to haunt the French imagination. The Beast preyed upon the country folk of the isolated Auvergne region of France. Descriptions of the devastation caused by the wolf, the werewolf, the hyena, or the man-like beast, as well as the fear it generated, have inspired numerous literary works, and even a recent movie replete with special effects.

The title of that movie is *The Brotherhood of the Wolf* (2001). It is often shown on late-night television. Directed by Christophe Gans, it stars Samuel Le Bihan as the naturalist Gregoire de Fronsac and Marc Dacascos as his friend and companion Mani, an improbably named Native Indian befriended by De Fronsac in New France. Mani is able to cast spells and farsee. He seems to understand the nature of the Beast. Maybe the creature of the movie, the Beast of Gévaudan, is in reality the "wild man" from the Lake of the Woods. If not, maybe the "wild man" will become the subject of just such a movie in the future.

Who knows?

(It is only fair to add that my speculations, which are based on Ritchie's speculations, which in turn are based on the anonymously written news item, weigh in at 207 words!)

THE BALDOON MYSTERY

The Baldoon Mystery is one of the earliest instances of a poltergeist at work and play in early Canada. It is especially interesting to us today because of the immense public interest it drew in its time, which is demonstrated by the detailed accounts that appeared in the newspapers of its day while the manifestations were occurring. Right from the first, sober-sided farmers and goggle-eyed visitors attested to the fact that strange things were happening at Baldoon.

A collection of anecdotal accounts of the disturbances and various theories as to their cause did appear, but no one has critically examined the events that took place at the McDonald farmhouse in the Scots settlement of Baldoon between 1829 and 1831, near present-day Wallaceburg, Ontario. But whenever a study of the phenomena does appear, it will make interesting reading.

Poltergeistery is a worldwide phenomenon marked by the absence of the ghost or spirit that is causing the disturbances. The locus of the manifestations is usually an unwitting teenage girl. Although there is no critical examination of the Baldoon Mystery, a lively drama has been devoted to it. The play, entitled *Baldoon*, was written by two poets, James Reaney and C.H. (Marty) Gervais, and catches the spirit (or spirits) of the time and place.

The article here, aside from the blather at the beginning, is a reasonable summary of some of the events that commenced in 1829 and continued for two years. The article is signed "Malcolm" but the writer's full name is unknown. He regarded himself as a skeptic, but he reveals himself to be uncritical, for he never allows a doubt to interrupt his telling of his tale.

"Unsolved Mystery" appeared in *The Globe* (Toronto), September 8, 1894. One characteristic of Malcolm's style is his long, involved sentences. The text is reprinted here as it appeared in the newspaper, except for the fact that the newspaper's long columns have been divided into paragraphs, a task the newspaper's editor neglected to undertake.

Unsolved Mystery

Haunted House of the Baldoon Settlement
A Tale of Forty Years Ago
Missiles Thrown by Unseen Hands
Beds that Rocked and Rose in the Air
Strange Behaviour of a Musket
Unaccountable Phenomena

(by Special Correspondent of *The Globe*)

Just at the present time, when the haunted schoolhouse in Grey is exciting attention, it seems proper to recall another mystery, which, happening more than 40 years ago, has never been satisfactorily explained, unless, indeed, we fall back on the ever-present doubt, inherent in us, all, that, despite our outward and often thrust forward scepticism, there may indeed be unseen forces around us — a spirit world in which we have no part, and of which we rarely witness manifestations.

For myself, I am a sceptic of sceptics — brought up by my Scotch ancestors to disbelieve in the existence of such phantoms — nay, trained rather to look on the discussion of which even to rank heresy, I entertain a well-grounded distrust of ghost stories in general, and for my own part have never seen anything to shake that prejudice. But when one converses with a man whose word has never been doubted, and he relates a circumstantial story of spooks with the matter-of-fact air which precludes doubt, it kind of staggers one's firm belief.

When, moreover, one inquires further and learns that a whole community, or the older people at least, implicitly believe this story, and that there are still several living witnesses, believable in all other affairs of life, it gives one's preconceived notions another and more severe jar, and one naturally questions himself: Can these things be true?

Such was my experience a few days ago in the pleasant Town of Wallaceburg, where I first heard of what has been called "The Baldoon Mystery" — a mystery which made much noise thereabouts some forty odd years ago. And first, let me tell you where Baldoon is.

At the beginning of the present century Lord Selkirk, in passing up our noble chain of lakes and rivers to his Red River settlement, noticed the beauty of a little peninsula, formed by the junction of the Sydenham and St. Clair Rivers. With an eye ever on the lookout for choice sites for his hardy Scotch settlers, he saw that this would be a splendid field for growing corn and other supplies for his colony scattered along the Red River of the north, for at that time it was supposed that none of the food grains could be grown so far north.

Just above the peninsula the green woods of Walpole Island — peopled then and now with dusky red men — divided the blue waters of the St. Clair and the current, clear and sparkling, which flowed past to meet the muddy Sydenham, had been christened by the early French explorers "Chenal Ecarté" — the lost channel, because it does not mix with the turbid Sydenham, but plunges under it, too proud to soil its lovely waters. This beautifully poetic name just now locally degenerated into the home-spun title of "The Sny," whatever that means.

Origin of Baldoon

At the "meeting of the waters," on the rich alluvial soil carried down by the two rivers, Lord Selkirk in 1804 founded the Baldoon settlement. On the extreme point of the peninsula, where the snow-flowing Sydenham met the limpid St. Clair, he erected a huge wind-mill, so that every field could be supplied with water, and on the Sydenham side extensive sheep-folds testified to the thrift of his settlers. Every season long boats, propelled slowly by oars called "batteaux," came down from the other settlement on the Red River, nearly a thousand miles away, and took back the surplus corn, wood, etc., of the Baldoon settlers.

Most of these settlers came from Argyleshire, and four family names were especially conspicuous, McDonalds, McDougalls, McGregors and McLeans. They had been specially chosen by Lord Selkirk for their physique and are described as models of womanly and manly beauty. At the present day their descendants, now scattered over a wide area, may be distinguished by their generous, open faces and lordly bearing. As the families intermarried and increased, it became difficult to distinguish the names apart, so that it was customary to call them "Farmer" McDonald, "Tailor" McDonald, etc., from their trade, or for any particularity, even.

Just outside the Baldoon settlement proper, and up the Chenal Ecarté about half a mile, there stood in 1829 a small log house, fronting the river, inhabited by a man named John McDonald, though he usually was called John "Tailor," as tailoring was his business, and many of his customers never knew that McDonald was his real name. This man was not from Argyleshire, like the other surrounding settlers, but from the islands of Arran off the Scottish coast. Subsequent developments caused his past history to be looked into rather carefully, but the most searching inquiries failed to descern anything discreditable.

Early in the spring of that year his modest little home acquired a notoriety, through strange manifestations which suddenly made their appearance. Perhaps the story may best be told by Mr. L.A. McDougall of Wallaceburg, a very old gentleman, but remarkably intelligent. Here it is as I gathered it from him a few days ago at his residence in the town:—

A Strange Story

"You are one of the original Baldoon settlers, I believe, Mr. McDougall?" I asked.

"No, not exactly, for I was born six years after my father settled there, and I am now 84," he answered, in the deep base of a Highlander.

"But you remember distinctly what was called the Baldoon mystery?" I persisted.

"Oh, yes; that was only about forty years ago" — as if forty years were only a slight gap.

"Would you mind telling me the particulars of that affair, Mr. McDougall?"

"Not at all, not at all," but turning quickly towards me, so that the light streamed full across his wrinkled but still handsome face. "Have you read the book they published about it some years ago?"

Upon my answer that I had not, he said, half to himself: "Just as well, just as well; most of it was lies, anyhow."

Then, settling himself back more comfortably in his chair, he resumed. "I was going up the river to Algonac one day that spring in my boat, with another man, and when we were opposite the tailor's house I noticed the women run out of the house screaming, as if frightened, and looking back again and again. We rowed into the shore, and asked them what was the matter. They said stones were coming in through windows. 'Stones?' we asked them again. 'Yes, stones from the bed of the river.' We ran over to the house and, sir, it was just as they said. Big and little stones were lying on the floor, and the windows all broken. While we were looking more stones came crushing through, and we ran outside to see who was throwing them, but there was not as much as a bush in front to hide in, and nobody in sight. The river, about half a mile wide, ran directly in front of the house."

"Did these stones come from any great force, Mr. McDougall?"

"Not particularly," he answered. "They broke the windows and rolled across to the opposite wall, where they lay in little heaps."

"Did you pick them up and examine them?"

"Oh, yes; they were the ordinary river stones of all shapes."

"Did you see any other uncanny signs then, Mr. McDougall?"

"Not at that time; but about two weeks after, hearing that they were still going on" — he invariably referred to the manifestations as "they" — "I went up and stopped over Sunday. The family had returned to the house, and I slept with one of the tailor's sons. During the night the bed began to wave back and forth in the air, as if we were at sea. My companion was sleeping soundly, so I woke him up and asked him did he feel the motion of the bed. He drowsily answered, 'Yes,' but said he was getting used to that sort of thing — that every night he heard carriages rolling across the roof before he went to sleep, and often the bed was up against the roof. In a short time he was again asleep, but I tell you I did not sleep much, for, besides the bed, once in a while a stone would come bang against the house."

There Was No Ghost

"Did you see anything ghostly, Mr. McDougall?" I asked.

"Nothing at all," he answered, "though I watched closely. We all went to church Sunday morning, and, coming home, one of the girls went ahead and unlocked the door of the house. Instantly she came screaming back to us, and on going up we found all the furniture, bedding, stoves and everything, piled up in a window from one corner to the other."

"How long did these things continue, Mr. McDougall?" I asked him.

"For nearly a year, and people came from Chatham and all over to see them go on," he answered. "The Catholics said that if a priest was brought he could stop them; but one did come from Chatham, and stayed for a week, but it was no use. They got worse, if anything, and the house began to get on fire, a dozen times a day, now, besides the stones. Many people took the lead balls, and, marking them, threw them out as far as they could in the river, but in a moment they would be back again in the room. At last they boarded up the windows, but as soon as a door was opened they came in there, and the house itself used to be bombarded day and night. One day a stranger came along on horseback — there were scarcely any taverns then — and asked the tailor could he stay all night. The tailor answered, yes, if he was not afraid of spirits. While they were talking at the door an old musket which hung on the opposite wall came down, and after going around the room it came and stood directly in front of the stranger's horse. 'If that's the kind of people you are, I'm away,' said the man in a frightened voice, as he drove the spurs into his horse."

"How did the people generally account for these things, Mr. McDougall?"

"Some said the tailor sold one of his children to the devil in the old country, but I never believed that story, for he always seemed a respectable, quiet man. Some others blamed a schoolmaster in Wallaceburg, and he lost his position through it, and went away, but they kept right on. At last, after the house had taken fire hundreds of times, they took out their furniture and let it burn down. They put up another, but it always could take fire day or night, and often right in the room where you were sitting the wall would blaze up. Finally, the tailor and his family moved to another house near Wallaceburg, but the same things happened — stones came through the windows, etc. — and they moved back again, as their landlord did not want them to remain."

"How did it end at last, Mr. McDougall?" I asked.

"It ended as suddenly as it began; they simply stopped themselves, and it became like any other house after a year of excitement."

Now, reader, you will naturally ask me, "Are these strange stories true?" That question I will not try to answer. You have them as I heard them from this courteous and respectable old gentleman, and draw your own conclusions. If at any time you visit the pretty little town of Wallaceburg, you can question for yourself; but, speaking generally, I may say this: they are usually believed there to be gospel truths, for they are vouched for by men of the highest standing. I may also add that one of "the tailor's" sons lives now in Marine City, Mich.

Malcolm.

THE GYPSY WOMAN AND THE LIZARDS

Here is a remarkably detailed account of how a gypsy woman cured a man of an unnamed, wasting disease. The incident is said to have occurred in Bathurst, N.B.

I would like to have more information about the gypsy woman in question. These days gypsies are known as the Rom or the Romany people. According to popular opinion, they originated in Egypt, but the truth is that the Gypsies migrated from India, where many of them are still to be found, to Eastern and Western Europe, and from there to the Americas. They constitute about 10 percent of the population of Romania. They are fabled for their fortune-telling, their curses, and their cures.

As for the lizards that are described here, they do not seem to be tapeworms, which thrive in the stomachs of the unwary and unlucky. Who knows what they are — or were.

"Extraordinary Affair" appeared in the *Constitutional* (St. Catharines), on July 28, 1864. The original spelling of "gipsey" has been retained. The reference to "St. John's" should read "Saint John." The lengthy column of type has been divided into paragraphs to render it easier to read.

Extraordinary Affair

(from *The Constitutional*)

The following extraordinary circumstance, which is said to have happened at Bathurst, near St. John's, New Brunswick, we find in the St. John's *Telegraph*. Its truth is vouched for, and the facts are related by a correspondent of that journal, under the date of July 1st, 1864:—

A farmer in this county, James Mulock, of the flat lands has been some three years confined to his bed, through weakness produced from emaciation; the cause of his sickness was unknown, and the symptoms bore no resemblance to any other disease that has appeared in this community. All the doctors have prescribed for him, and all with the same result — complete failure.

A few weeks ago, however, a gipsey woman, who has been telling fortunes for some time past, offered to cure him for $100, the sum to be placed in the hands of Mr. Ferguson, who was to be the judge of the cure; Mulock was to put himself completely in her hands, and leave his home for one week. He did so although his wife demurred to the arrangement, and tried to persuade him from it; he however persisted, and went with her, accompanied by his younger brother Charles, and now we may as well take the story of the latter:—

"We went with her to her camp; immediately after entering we had some bread and ham; Jim and I both eating heartily. After dinner the gipsey said she wished to speak with me alone. I went into the woods back from the camp, when she at once asked me if I was willing that Jim should be hand-cuffed and his feet bound, and to submit altogether to her. I said I was not. Then, said she, it's no use wasting words about the matter; if you don't do so he'll never be cured. I asked her to explain herself; she said she would not. I at last consented thinking to myself there can be nothing wrong while I am here.

"At tea we had some salt pork fried, and some good bread. Next morning on waking, after a very watchful night, for I never closed my eyes, I found Jim completely tied up. He seemed rather put out, but the gipsey told him at once that she had done so, because he had to suffer a good deal of pain before being cured. I assented to this. He said he was willing to go through with it since he had begun.

"We had breakfast, salt pork and bread. I fed Jim, and we laughed at the farce, as we considered it, not having faith in her. After breakfast I talked with the gipsey, and asked her what she meant; I told her I was no child, and must either know her plans or I would unloose Jim and go home again. She then told me she knew that Jim had some living reptile in him, and the only way to cure him was to feed him with salt food for a day or two, and then to stop him from drinking altogether, when the animal would come out to seek water. She said she had cured others, but I must expect to see him suffer awful pain and torture when his drink was completely stopped, but it would only be for 24 or 30 hours.

"I went to Jim, told him all, and asked him if he was willing to undergo it. Says he, 'Charley, that woman has it; I'll stand it.'

"Well, that day passed, salt pork and bread, and to Jim a very limited supply of water; the next day the same, till after dinner, when the water was altogether stopped. Now commenced the work. He begged and prayed for water, he howled till he was hoarse; the woman then gave him a drink of what I considered water, but which she told me afterwards was salt pork fat, melted; he drank it in a few mouthfuls, and in a few minutes more he was worse than ever. He begged me to shoot him, to drown him, to do anything with him, only not leave him in that state.

"Towards evening he became quite out of his mind; water and springs was all he raved about. He lay that way for some time, almost until morning, when he got into a high fever. I got alarmed, and told the gipsey I thought it had gone far enough, that Jim was too weak to stand it. She told me I could do as I liked, but if I would leave him two hours longer I would see whether she or the doctors were right. She likewise told him that if he loosed, he would kill himself drinking at the first water he came to. I tried her.

"In about an hour after, she asked me to drag him to the spring, a few rods away from the camp. We got him inside it. She laid his head with his lips almost touching the water; she took up a birth pannikin and commenced lifting up water and letting it fall just before his lips. He was all this time as quiet as if he was dead; sometimes he gave a slight shiver; his mouth was wide open, and his eyelids opened and shut, the white of the eyes only being seen.

"After about ten minutes she said to me, 'Now who's right? but keep quiet.' I leaned over, and saw a large green lizard peeping out of his mouth; it did not seem as if it wanted to come out, but drew itself in again. 'It will come out again,' says the gipsey. While she was speaking two lizards glided out of his mouth into the water; the gipsey quietly killed one with a small stick, and I killed the other. We waited again for five minutes, when three came out, but not together. These we killed, although one almost escaped from the water to his mouth ere it was completely dispatched. We then waited nearly an hour longer, but no more made their appearance.

"The gipsey then said, 'There is no more,' and proceeded to pour water on Jim's forehead. She did so twenty minutes; she then gave him about a teaspoonful of water to drink; it actually hissed in his mouth. She kept him confined that day and half the next before she let him free, gradually increasing his allowance of water."

Such is the story told by Mr. Charles Mulock, and although I am not personally acquainted with the gentleman, I am told that he is one of the last men in the country to tell a wilful untruth. One fact, however, is clear — his brother has completely recovered his health, and not only his health, but his flesh, and now weighs 160 lbs., his former weight being only 73 lbs. This difference has been added in less than nine weeks. The lizards are of a bottle-green colour, about 5 inches long, red eyes and forked tongues.

There is a peculiarity about them different from the rest of the lizard tribe, their being only two feet, and sloping from thence in a wedge shape into a tail. Two of them have been preserved in spirits and forwarded to Prof. Agassiz, of Harvard University. One is preserved in spirits and kept in Mr. Ferguson's office, and the other two were forwarded to Professor Jack, who has written to a legal gentleman here, to say that those are the only specimens he ever met with, with the exception of one, found in the University of Munich, that is called the *Lacerta homo* in the language of the schools, and the Munich specimen was supposed to be the only one extant, although it was well known to the ancients.

He thinks that Mr. Mulock must have received them in an embryonic state by some of those mysterious secrets that are found in every path of science. A species, he says, corresponding to it, is unknown to live on land, and all naturalists have agreed that it requires the local action of the human stomach to produce it. This is, he says, the only explanation that can be offered that is not unphilosophical.

HAVE CLOTHES GHOSTS?

The subject of this essay — the garb of the ghost — is a curious one, one that is treated in an unexpected way. The relationship between ghosts and their clothing, a puzzling one, is given treatment that is inventive and light-hearted. It comes from an unexpected source, the *Evening News* (St. John's, Newfoundland), on March 18, 1869.

The essay is unsigned. I wish I knew who wrote it. If I did, I would search out more essays by him (or her).

The subject is not as silly as at first it might seem. Psychical researchers in the late nineteenth and early twentieth centuries long marvelled that ghosts traditionally appeared as gaunt figures wearing flowing white gowns, rather like Ancient Greeks or members of the Ku Klux Klan! Perhaps the garb goes back to the long cloaks worn by the alchemists of the Middle Ages, though a more likely suggestion is that the garb recalls the cerements or "winding sheets" used for the burial of the dead in the past and in Near Eastern countries to this day.

The essay ends with a reference to a fashionable style of dress and comportment now consigned to the past. "Grecian bend" is a period style described in one fashion text as "an affectation in walking assumed by English ladies in 1875." Women affecting it balanced on high heels and carried the upper part of the body inclined forward. As one commentator noted, "The silliness spread to America and other countries which affect passing oddities of fashions." It is indeed hard to imagine how a ghost, a weightless entity, could or would affect the "Grecian bend."

Have Clothes Ghosts?

(from *The Evening News*)

Have clothes ghosts? What a question! exclaims the reader. Well, then, did you ever hear of a naked ghost? Never. In every well-authenticated instance, the ghost who appeared to the affrighted eyes of the observer was clothed in some style or other. There was the ghost of the little old bald-headed man in blue coat with brass buttons, in short breeches and black stockings, with spectacles on his nose, who walked sadly around in his old office or bedroom, as though something was on his mind. If we remember rightly, his appearance led to a careful examination among the secret drawers of his old secretary desk, and his long-secreted will was discovered, and with it the paper that showed that the mortgage upon the homestead was cancelled, and his distressed heirs were made happy. Then there was the pale-faced, sickly-looking lady, in deep mourning, who had mysteriously disappeared, but who could not rest quiet in her grave, and who pointed to a particular spot in the garden, beneath which her remains were discovered, and with them the proof that she had been murdered for her money, that led to the execution of her guilty nephew, who confessed the deed and died duly penitent, while her own bones were deposited in consecrated ground, and she walked no more.

The number of ghosts who have walked in long, white grave clothes is innumerable. There have been ghosts in ordinary military garb, and ghosts in suits of armour, and ghosts apparelled as monks and nuns, and ghosts who clanked rattling chains, and ghosts clad in the habiliments of every walk and rank of life — but never a naked ghost.

How is this? What was the nature of their clothing? Ghost and clothing have been alike transparent and intangible. Both could be seen, and yet seen through. The chair or table, the fire-place or the trees behind them could be distinctly perceived, and as they passed the window through which the moonbeams shone they cast no shadow. Some even have been palpable, as those upon whom their cold, cold, clammy hands were laid most thrillingly can testify. But they are clothed, all of them. That do we know, and that only do we propose to consider.

Why should ghosts be clothed? In the warm quarters provided for the souls of the wicked dead, is clothing needed, or is the propriety of use regarded? In Heaven, from whence good ghosts sometimes come, we learn that spirits are clad in shining raiment and white robes. These then may be the clothes that they bring with them. Spiritualists and clairvoyants who see more than other people have even undertaken to describe minutely the apparel worn in another world, saying that it was of all the colours of the rainbow, and fashioned solely in accordance with the taste and liking of the wearer. But we propose not to meddle with such questions, for we know nothing of them.

Yet one fact is clear: Since ghosts come not naked upon earth, but are always clothed, clothes have their ghosts as well as men. The old blue coat and the snuff-coloured breeches that the ancient merchant wore in his lifetime must have had their own ghosts, else how could they have appeared in company with their former owners? The ponderous armour of the ancient knight, the widow's weeds, the clanking chains, and the trailing sheet that scared the observer who awake with chilled blood and a sudden start as the apparition stood by his bedside, had their ghosts as well as the dead whose sad and warning face he saw and recognized, and whose long, thin hand was so menacingly stretched out over him. They existed, they were sought and found, and the man-ghost clad himself in these ghostly habiliments that his identity might be distinguished.

What a field for speculation is here opened up! Men have their ghosts, and may return again. My old coat, and your old hat, my sister's chignon and my wife's hooped petticoat, my father's old gray wig and my mother's old bonnet, and your daughter's small and more fashionable one — so small that it is sometimes doubtful whether it is a bonnet or a mere head-dress — each have their several ghosts, and may again appear when discarded, and be visible to mortal eyes as part and parcel of their present wearers. Would that the Grecian bend was already among the ghosts. Can any body imagine a ghost in a Grecian bend?

Dear ladies, if my theory is true (and deny it who can?) who is it among you that would be willing to appear and be known in history hereafter as the fair ghost in a Grecian bend?

CHINESE SUPERSTITION

Political correctness is one characteristic of present-day newspapers that was not found in newspapers of the past. In many respects newspapermen of the nineteenth century could draw on wider vocabularies than can communicators in the twenty-first century. We should not project our sensitivities to slurs and slights onto innocent people and find them where they were never meant to be.

Here is an astonishing story about "fire-angels" that is only one paragraph long. But it says a lot about the people from China who came to British Columbia to work on the railway. What was said then would not be said (in this way, anyway) today. The word "Chinaman" is no longer acceptable; a reference to people from China as "Celestials" is old hat; slighting beliefs is not the done thing these days.

This news item titled "Chinese Superstition" comes from the *Cariboo Sentinel*, Barkersville, British Columbia, July 24, 1869:

> Chinese Superstition— Yesterday a Chinaman, who appears to be an intelligent Celestial, informed us that two Chinamen who were near Quesnel river when the forest fire took place on Tuesday last, saw two men dressed in red descend from the clouds. Fearful of the fire, the two mundane Celestials besought the fire-angels to take them under their protection, which they declined doing, and then suddenly disappeared. We do not know whether Chinamen indulge much in fabricating what we denominate "canards" or not, but it is quite certain that they are much given to the fabrication of all kinds of statements not in accordance with facts, and therefore the above statement about the fire-angels may

or may not be taken as a "sell." The Celestial, however, appeared to be in earnest about the fire-angels, and in confirmation of his belief in the statement of the two men who report having seen them, said that when there was a large fire in Canton a thousand fire-angels descended to the earth, all dressed in red, and set fire to the city in a thousand places, burning a great many people. Water was powerless to quench the fire where a fire-angel appeared, and it was useless to attempt doing so until he had gone away. We understand that this belief in the origin and continuation of fires through the agency of angels is quite common among the Chinese.

STRANGE TALE OF HORRORS

Poltergeists are known by their effects, not their appearances.

Whenever an old house is described as "haunted," it is generally the machinations of a noisy and disembodied spirit that is referred to, not a full-bodied ghost. Poltergeists make mischief, and more, in halls, corridors, rooms, closets, attics, and cellars. (I have yet to read or hear of a haunted outhouse.)

"Strange Tale of Horrors," a highly readable account of disturbances that took place in a house in Toronto, appeared in *The Globe* (Toronto) on January 15, 1886. Although the news story is reported in the third person, it includes a lively, verbatim account from the boarder who was most affected by the disturbances. This compound of dull objectivity and bouncy subjectivity in reporting, interesting in itself, has become characteristic of most of the writing that is done in this field these days.

Three other points are of interest. The newspaperman cannot resist the temptation to interject himself into the story, suggesting that there is little that is truly objective and non-partisan about the telling of a good story. Then there is the matter of whether or not a house is devalued if it has a reputation of being a haunt. Does including in a news story the street address of the house effectively lower its resale value? Realtors today speak of houses with such reputations as being "stigmatized." There is no discussion in this matter, yet Mr. Nie, the agent, obviously has this in mind — as well as a vested interest in scotching any rumours that something is "wrong" with the property.

The final point is the fact that this haunted house and any other such places in the city might well have influenced a young remittance man who settled in Toronto in 1890 and spent two years in the city. That man went on to write tales of terror set in haunted houses. Algernon Blackwood is his name, and it is not unlikely that he took accounts like these and wove their details and their drama into his widely published stories.

Strange Tale of Horrors
Experiences in a House Said to Be "Haunted"
Bells Ringing, Bolted Doors Banging,
Winds Where There Should Be No Wind,
Inmates almost Paralyzed with Fear,
And a Pandemonium of Unaccountabilities

(from *The Globe*)

There have been some strange goings on at a house on Gerrard street West lately. The house used to be occupied by an old couple, who owned it, and at their demise it fell into the hands of agents. The old people were always very mysterious, and spent the life of hermits while they lived, never seeing anyone or hardly ever allowing themselves to be seen. Since they died the house remained vacant until about a month ago, when a gentleman named Mr. Farrel rented it. He occupied the basement, and advertised the upper part for rent as "vacant rooms." It had been rumoured the place was haunted, but neither he nor his wife knew anything about it when they went in. The rooms are connected throughout with call bells, and, in the middle of the night, he would be rudely awakened by the violent ringing of these bells. Then he would hear the doors rattle and bang while

Heavy Footsteps Were Heard

across the rooms upstairs. Of course he was convinced someone was in the house, but on investigation he would find that everything was securely locked and quiet, just as he had left it when he retired. He was not a believer in ghosts, and would lay the unseemly noises to his imagination and returned to bed and to sleep only to be again aroused to consciousness by hearing the back door bang back and forth at a tremendous rate. Thinking it was open he would arise to shut it, but mystery of mysteries, it was found shut and locked, just as he had left it on retiring for the night. He thought these occurrences rather strange, but did not pay much attention to them for a night or two, and, in the meantime, a widow lady and her daughter rented the vacant part of the house and moved in. They slept one night in the house, or rather stayed awake one night in the house, and moved out as rapidly as possible the next day. A *Globe* reporter, happening to hear of the affair, called on the ladies, who said:— "God forbid that we should spend such another night as the one we spent in that place. We had

An Unaccountable Weird Feeling

as soon as night fell. We had a roaring fire going all the time, but still we shivered. We seemed to imagine all kinds of strange things. We retired, not very well assured, at last, to bed, but not to sleep. Something mysterious seemed to be weighing on the atmosphere. At last nature asserted her rights, and we dozed off to sleep. About half-past eleven a fearful banging commenced downstairs; we started up in bed and listened; yes, we were sure the door downstairs was open. Then, although the room was all closed and situated so that a breath of wind could not come through it, the

Wind Blew Over the Bed

at a terrific rate, raising up the bed-clothes. One of us jumped out of bed and called to Mr. Farrel downstairs to shut the back door; but he seemed bewildered, and would not say whether it was open or shut. We had just settled down again when there came a crack just outside the room door, and a shadow flitted across the foot of the bed followed by the sound of heavy footsteps in the hall. Then the front door rattled and creaked as though it were turning on its hinges to admit someone. We were almost dead with fright, and our teeth were chattering at a great rate, but still we could not pluck up courage to call out for fear we would be laughed at for our foolish imaginations.

We quieted ourselves best we could and tried to sleep, but no use; the noises kept recurring. Then

The Wall Paper

in the next room, which had just been put on two days before, began to roll off the walls as if it were alive, and almost frightened us out of our senses. We firmly resolved that if ever we saw daylight we would lose no time in moving out, although we had to lose a month's rent. We don't doubt but that our excited imaginations created some of the alarms, but no one can deny there were most unaccountable noises, and just let anyone who is skeptical spend one night in the room we did. We were thankful when morning came, and lost no time in getting out." The reporter visited the house, and saw the wall paper rolled off the walls, which Mr. Farrel was replacing. He said on Tuesday that he would not sleep another night in the place. Several neighbours were spoken to, and all seemed to be greatly excited over the affairs, which is considered quite a sensation.

A Contradiction

Mr. Nie, agent of the house in question, was seen, and says that the statements made concerning it are untrue. The house belongs to a widow, who left it some seven weeks ago after residing in it for several years, the last year and a half with only her three children. The house was the residence for many years of the late Dr. Rolph.

CLAIRVOYANT PHYSICIAN

The concept of "evidence-based medicine" was developed by David Guyatt, professor of Medicine and Clinical Epidemiology and Biostatistics at McMaster University in Hamilton, Ontario. The term itself was coined by Dr. Guyatt, and it first appeared in print in one of his hospital bulletins in 1990. It has caught on like wildfire. Its use is an attempt to make a distinction between tested, scientific medical practices and untested forms of traditional therapies. As important as it is, the concept is a controversial one. Within the medical establishment, reservations are expressed, given that there have been so few scientific trials; within the circles of alternative practitioners, resentments are expressed because of dismissal of experience with time-honoured therapies.

It is important to remember that medical science is fairly new, whereas traditional healing practices are hoary with age. Non-conventional treatments continue to abound.

Here is a short, curious, untitled item from the columns of the *New Brunswick Reporter*, December 15, 1883. At the time it was written, physicians were duly licensed, but by contemporary standards, medical training and licensing standards were lax. Even so, when I first read this account, I was extremely doubtful about the truth of the statement that appears in the last paragraph — that New Brunswick's *Medical Act* recognizes "clairvoyant physicians."

There are two other points of present-day interest. The description of Dr. Smith's practice recalls that of a later, famous American practitioner, Edgar Cayce, "the sleeping prophet," who would fall into a trace state and clairvoyantly diagnose patients. The examination of "a lock of hair" does have a contemporary ring to it. It seems to allude to the DNA sampling of forensic and other scientists.

The doubts that I harboured about the medical status of "clairvoyant physicians" led me to draft a letter about the matter and post it to the registrar of the College of Physicians and Surgeons of New Brunswick. In the letter I inquired about the professional status of Drs. Smith and Pomroy, and also about the special status of clairvoyants.

In short order, I received an admirably detailed letter of response from Ed Schollenberg, MD, LLB, FRCPC, registrar of the college. In his reply, dated March 26, 2003, Dr. Schollenberg wrote as follows:

> First of all, I would like to say that I can find no evidence that either Dr. Smith or Dr. Pomroy were ever licensed as physicians here. Nor can I find any specific provision which would license "Clairvoyant" physicians.

Dr. Schollenberg went on to add some intriguing details about the practice of medicine at the time:

> By way of background, prior to 1881, the regulation of medicine in New Brunswick was rather loose, despite some provincial legislation. In 1881, the *Medical Act* was passed which basically followed that which had been undertaken elsewhere. It did grandfather existing physicians and attempted to mandate all to be licensed. It is not clear whether they all did as there was no huge advantage to being licensed. Furthermore, it seems some did object to the annual fee, then about a dollar. Hence, it is theoretically possible that Dr. Smith and Dr. Pomroy were practising prior to 1881 and simply didn't bother to register.
>
> Having said that, we do have a copy of the Medical Register of the day, commencing with 1881. Neither of their names are on that.
>
> Furthermore, I can find no reference to either of them in the book *Medicine in New Brunswick* by Dr. Stewart. This is probably the most complete historiography on early physicians in New Brunswick.

So it is unlikely that either Smith or Pomroy was a physician. What about the status of clairvoyants as recognized medical practitioners? Here again Dr. Schollenberg is definitive:

> Regarding the question whether there was a specific provision for "Clairvoyants," I can not find such in the *Medical Act* around that time. It is known that legislation in both Upper and Lower Canada, prior to Confederation, did grant special status to two groups, specifically "homeopaths" and "eclectics." This was to protect them from prosecution by orthodox physicians and, in fact, granted them specific representation on governing bodies. Nevertheless, I can find no specific status granted to any other group, nor any mention in Hamowy's book on early regulation of medicine in Canada.
>
> It is possible that there was some obscure legislation passed at some point around that time by the New Brunswick legislature. This could be searched with some difficulty. My suspicion is, however, that such does not exist as there is no further reference to it in any subsequent legislation.

No doubt Dr. Schollenberg is right.

It seems to me quite likely that "Dr." Smith and "Dr." Pomroy were practising "homeopaths" or "eclectics." Such healers were plentiful during the nineteenth century; indeed homeopathy, which is based on the administration of minute doses of substances, is even more popular in the twenty-first century than it ever was in the nineteenth. Eclectic healers are less commonly encountered today, for they selected treatment modalities from the disciplines of the past and combined them, sometimes with the marvel of the age: electricity.

I have explored this matter at some length because it illustrates the fact that one cannot take on faith statements made in print, even in the columns of *The New Brunswick Reporter*!

Clairvoyant Physician

(from *The New Brunswick Reporter*)

Geo. W. Smith, Clairvoyant Physician, since the fire at the Queen Hotel, may now be consulted at the Commercial Hotel, York Street, Fredericton. His method of examination is not generally known except to those who have had the benefit of his services, of whom there are many in this City who can testify to his powers. Whilst examining a patient either personally or by a lock of hair he is entranced and entirely unconscious of what takes place either at the time of the examination or afterwards, unless told by the parties. Some of his most remarkable cases have been treated by him by a lock of hair without ever having seen the patient personally, many of them living in distant parts of this Province and some in the Province of Nova Scotia. The accuracy of his diagnosis of entire strangers and persons not present or known at all to him, is most wonderful and has given the greatest satisfaction to those most interested in it. Whatever doubts some persons may entertain of his gift or from whatever source it comes, anyone who consults him must acknowledge the very great accuracy with which, when entranced, he can describe their feelings and bodily ailments whatever they may be, this too without having had the slightest previous communication with the party; and if they follow his directions they will be surprised to find how simple a remedy will remove the cause of years of suffering. The Doctor prefers that nothing should be said to him about their ailments before examination either by the patients or any one else, and when hair is sent it should be cut near the head and should not be handled by any person except the patient if possible.

Dr. Smith is a native of New Brunswick, having been born at St. David's, in the County of Charlotte, and is a descendant of one of the old Loyalists. He is one of the Clairvoyant Physicians legally authorized by the medical act of New Brunswick to practise in this Province. Dr. Pomroy also, as well known throughout the Dominion, is another.

A HAUNTED HOUSE

In the past, houses were well and truly haunted, and we have newspaper reports to prove it. In those days, journalists would relish the task of describing all manner of ghostly manifestations based on interviews conducted with no end of witnesses. Space was not at a premium, and accounts were surprisingly detailed. Seldom would journalists search for a cause or a resolution of a "mystery."

"Haunted" is such an article. It appeared in the *Victoria Daily Colonist*, August 5, 1886. It describes manifestations that would lead a psychical researcher to suggest that there is a poltergeist (or "noisy ghost") at work, except for the fact that there is the description of "a tall man … with shoulders slightly bent" who "would vanish, only, however, to appear again."

It is unlikely that one of today's broadsheet-sized newspapers would publish an account like this one, though a tabloid-sized paper might, and there are television programs like *Unexplained Mysteries* and *Sightings* that would claim it as their own, complete with special effects, both sound and light.

I find myself wondering what became of this "large and commodious house" on Cormorant Street. And of the restless spirit of the man who may have haunted it over a century ago!

Haunted

The Strange and Unaccountable Sounds
Heard in House on Cormorant Street

The Shade of Mortal Appears at Intervals
and Existence of a Hidden Crime

(from the *Victoria Daily Colonist*)

About four months ago a married couple rented a "large and commodious house" on Cormorant Street, and furnished it with the intention of letting apartments. They had not long been installed in their new quarters before they began to be

Disturbed at Night by Peculiar Sounds

proceeding from the inside of the house. Doors which had been fast locked would bang in the middle of a still night, and being inspected, would be seen to be secure. Retiring to rest the inmates would be disturbed a moment later by a repetition of the same sounds, and a further quest would fail to reveal anything. Then again foot-steps walking through the hall and different rooms of the house were occasionally heard, not only at night, but in the day time. The sounds and noises, though frequent, were not then, however, regular, but this defect, if whatever it may be called, has since been entirely remedied, for, since two weeks ago and up to the present time, only one night has passed without a manifestation of some kind being given. The most frequently repeated experience is for the inmates — comprising sometimes the tenants, sometimes the lodgers, and occasionally both — to suddenly hear footsteps, apparently those of a man, upon the front stoop. The door is then seemingly opened

And Closed with a Bang That Shakes the House

before any one can get into the hall to see if the process actually takes place or the sounds only — but not too late to hear the foot-steps pass by and down the hall — though nothing is visible. The steps always die away about twelve feet from the door at the rear end of the hall, and all remains quiet for perhaps half an hour, when the same thing again takes place. This is, to say the least, not pleasant, but it is, also, not all.

A Few Nights Ago,

when the time was drawing towards morning, the mistress of the house was aroused by a breeze such as would be produced by a fanning motion, and in awakening, did so with the impression that hands had been quietly laid upon her face. Though not of a nervous temperament she was naturally somewhat disturbed, and her agitation was not allayed on hearing a number of deliberate taps on the wall or window. Hastily attiring herself, she knocked at the room door of the then only other person in the house and requested him to dress himself. Upon doing so they adjourned to the sitting room, but had hardly entered when the

Click of a Pistol

— or what seemed like it — proceeding from the bedroom, where a light had been left burning, was distinctly heard by both, which made their flesh creep, as it would that of many brave persons. Several lodgers, frightened to stay, have left the house; and among their number was one who shared in a still more striking experience. The landlady was in the kitchen when she suddenly

Became Conscious That Someone Was Standing Behind Her

and half turning, saw a tall man, apparently about 36 or 38 years of age, with shoulders slightly bent, dark hair brushed back from his forehead which narrowed somewhat as it advanced, face shaven excepting the moustache, and eyes, whose color she could not determine, wearing a look that she describes as "startled." Upon looking directly at it, it would vanish, only, however, to appear again. Believing herself the victim of an excited imagination she refrained from relating her experience; but that night the noises and footsteps doubled in intensity. The lodger, who had also been awakened, arose and came into the hall, pale as a sheet, where he was shortly after joined by the landlady. With a strange expression on his face he asked her if she had seen anybody besides himself in the house that night, and upon being questioned, he stated that as he came out of his room into the hall he

Saw the Figure of a Man Standing in the Hall

near the spot where the footsteps generally cease, and, upon describing the appearance, the landlady found that it tallied with the vision she herself had witnessed. Last Saturday during the day as well as the evening the door rattled and slammed, and footsteps passed through the hall in rapid succession — that is to say the whole process was frequently repeated, but in such a vigorous manner as to suggest that the uncanny visitant was getting impatient. Those sounds were heard by the husband and wife and two others, but nothing could be detected, and, in spite of the utmost vigilance, the sound of a footstep on the front door — even to the jar of the boot against the threshold — the grasping, opening, and slamming of the door, and the sound of heavy walking in the passage continued to be heard; and so on throughout the night. On this day, for the first time, the sound had come to the back door which responsively shook and banged, while the footsteps of the restless walker were again heard in the hall. On Sunday last all was quiet until the evening

When the Sounds Re-Commenced

with such loudness as to awaken all in the house — and keep them awake, too.

On Monday afternoon a lady visitor was sitting in the parlor when the same thing again happened. A step was heard outside — the front door seemed to open and shut — and, not wishing to meet the husband until she should be introduced to him by the wife, the lady rose from her seat, passed through the bedroom, kitchen, and into the wash-house where her hostess was, the steps proceeding down the hall, but in this case the walker was heard to stagger as though wounded — or drunk. On the bedroom floor

Is a Large Stain

of what may, or may not, be blood.

No theory of the mystery is advanced, and we merely relate what have been vouched for as actual occurrences. As a proof that the tenants are at least in earnest, it may be mentioned that they have given notice to leave what they may be excused for regarding as a haunted house.

B.C. CANNIBALS

This news story makes for grisly reading, though it is not about grizzly bears but about cannibalistic practices that took place not in darkest Africa but on the West Coast of Canada. It is hardly suitable reading for each and every night of the year, so it should be set aside to be read on a night like Halloween.

"B.C. Cannibals" appeared in the *Free Press* (Winnipeg, Manitoba) on September 27, 1889. What to make of it? Is the account factual? It is certainly sensationally written and a hostile reaction to the known cannibalistic practices of the Indians of the West Coast. Whether those practices were current in the 1880s is a moot point. The writer, who remains unidentified, seems not to have witnessed any of the ceremonies at which human flesh was said to be devoured, but many of his informants claimed they were witnesses to these practices and described for him the bloody feasts. Yet the writer does hedge his bets: "If this was not human flesh both he and the whole audience were deceived."

What is being described is the winter initiation ceremony of the Hamatsa secret society of the Kwakitul of the West Coast. For four days and nights, elaborately masked dancers performed ritual ceremonies to appease the Cannibal at the North End of the World. It was an impressive ceremony known to be symbolic in form and content, though it is not hard to imagine that in the past performances involved the consumption of raw human flesh. To add to the drama, one of the dancers would "go mad" on cue and perform "for real."

Today one might liken the performance to that of "psychic surgery," whereby the would-be surgeon creates the illusion that he is making incisions in the human body, drawing blood, and removing "obstructions," all without any pain and without leaving a scar.

One also thinks of the manager of a movie theatre in Texas who thought he would add a note of terror to a midnight showing of the horror film *The Texas Chainsaw Massacre* by running up and down the aisles with a roaring chainsaw! There was panic in the house.

The writer has no use for cannibalism (who does?) but he also dismisses the potlatch ceremony as an "orgy," thereby displaying a lack of sympathy for Native customs generally.

B.C. Cannibals
Horrible Practices of Degraded Indians
in Far Northwestern Wilds
Victoria Letter in St. Paul Globe

(from *The Free Press*)

The British Columbia Indians have been suspected of eating human flesh, but they have hitherto concealed their practices so carefully that no reliable white man is able to give personal testimony of the fact. H.R.A. Pocock has been spending a great deal of time among them, and, although he is not able to give personal testimony of their cannibalistic rites, yet he collected a great deal of evidence from the natives of the prevalence of the practice.

The Kwagutis, a tribe dwelling in the central part of the province, have a belief that if a man meets a certain spirit on the mountains he has a right thereafter during the winter dances, lasting two months of the year, to bite whoever displeases him. The spirit is called. They belong to what may be called an exclusive and aristocratic caste. Only members of certain families may become Ha-mad-tsis, and these when they come to the years of discretion go up into the mountains, where they may meet the spirit. Having encountered this unlovely spirit they come back to the villages snapping and biting at everybody, and making themselves generally undesirable neighbours. Their sole purpose is to show the tribe that they are different from ordinary men, and do not care what they eat or what they suffer. In old times a captive or a slave was killed and presented to the initiated, who ate the corpse in the presence of a general assemblage of the people. More recently, although slavery is not wholly extinct, the Indians have become afraid to kill, so they are reduced to the stealing of corpses. Usually these have been drying for a long time, being "buried" among the branches of a tree, and are quite flavourless, the brains alone being considered a luxury.

Up to the time of eating a corpse in public the acolyte, whenever he appears from the woods, bites indiscriminately, women being, however, generally exempt, whether from native gallantry or not does not appear. Formerly the faces were bitten, noses and ears especially, but the cannibal now merely lifts the flesh of a man's arm with his teeth, which is sliced off with a knife by a bystander, while the half insane savage retains his grip of it, and finally swallows it. The father of the biter pays everybody who has suffered from his progeny's enthusiasm from two to ten blankets. There are few men in the Kwaguti tribes who do not bear the scar of this extraordinary mania. The Ha-mad-tsis, during the progress of the winter dances, is stark naked, a heavy plaited rope of cedar bark, adorned with tassels being carried, however, on the sholders. There are from three to twenty Ha-mad-tsis, and each of them will perhaps eat of four or five corpses in a lifetime. Mr. Pocock, however, had one old gentleman pointed out to him who had partaken of twenty. At the same time, the corpse is frequently a sham one made up for the purpose. Deer or goat flesh is often tied to human bones and devoured in the dusk, so that the onlookers are all deceived. Still there are no doubt well authenticated cases of this species of emotional ceremonial cannibalism constantly taking place among these degraded slaves in the interior. Mr. Pocock has not actually witnessed the ceremony, but he collected a considerable amount of testimony from what he considers reliable native witnesses. He says:

"My interpret said that when he was a lad he remembers his mother saving two slaves from being killed and eaten. The winter or Ha-mad-tsis dance was performed at Alert Bay eighteen months ago, goat's flesh being eaten from human bones at midnight and the tribe deceived. Apparently two bodies were devoured at Klawatis that same season. Three and a half years ago a white man was taken by his Indian woman to the winter dance and turned out of doors beside, as the woman told him, a corpse was to be eaten. He saw a woman's body taken into the house by three naked men, and went round the back, where, through a hole, he saw the Ha-mad-tsis holding the body in their arms and biting pieces out. From the long black hair hanging from what seemed to be the head he supposed this was the body of a woman. If this was not human flesh both he and the whole audience were deceived.

"A Fort Rupert half-breed woman of excellent character told me she was fully convinced that in many cases no deception was practised. No half-breeds or Indians except my interpreter expressed any doubt. A Kanaka, a man of good report indeed, told me that at the head of Knight Inlet he was admitted to a winter war dance and saw three Ha-mad-tsis eat a corpse in presence of the tribe. The evidence appears to me to be conclusive on account of the witness' character and the clearness and reasonable manner of his statements. He told me his story briefly, and as one surprised at the existence of doubt, but tired of the subject. His wife, a member of the Ha-mad-tsis family, furnished the evidence that convinced my interpret that the Ha-mad-tsis is not a sham.

"After describing the origin of the rite in her family she said that some years ago, on Knight Inlet, at the winter feasts, she was invited to a feast of berries for women. They were interrupted by the Ha-mad-tsis bringing a human corpse into the house. They were six in number, and all naked, and her brother was one of them. Attendants cut off strips of flesh from the corpse, which were devoured by the Ha-mad-tsis. This witness, although given to potlatching, another heathen, and forbidden semi-religious orgy, bore otherwise a good character. I was told a number of most horrible stories of self-torture practised out of bravado during these ceremonies."

REMARKABLE DREAMS

David Boyle (1842–1911) was a self-taught archaeologist with a passion for the past. Born in Greencock, Scotland, he was brought to this country as a child and at the age of fourteen was apprenticed as a blacksmith. He educated himself and became a school principal in Elora, Ontario, before he was able to direct his energies toward his life's ambition to be a museum curator and archaeologist. Indeed, he became Canada's premier archaeologist. All his life he was enthusiastic about the discovery, examination, preservation, and protection of the antiquities of Ontario, be they objects like bones or arrowheads, Algonkian legends and myths, or farmers' customs, beliefs, and practices.

Among his other achievements, David Boyle was a lively writer. Reproduced here are two dreams that he included in one of the columns devoted to "Canadian Folk-Lore" that appeared in *The Globe* (Toronto) on Saturdays between November 1897 and March 1898. They were widely read and occasioned much interesting mail from readers. The excerpt reproduced here comes from a column devoted to the subject of spirits, which appeared on May 5, 1898.

The Globe of Boyle's day became *The Globe and Mail* of our day. It is a shame the newspaper does not commission columns as serious, stylish, and enlightening as Boyle's. There is nothing in any contemporary Canadian paper to match this series. In this column, the writer noted that the previous week's column caught the eye of "a Toronto gentleman," someone who in the practice of the times could remain nameless. The gentleman in question described two of his dreams. The first dream was an anticipation of the assassination of Thomas D'Arcy McGee, which occurred in downtown Ottawa on April 7, 1868. The second dream was also prophetic, for it offered specific details as to the death of a dear friend.

I try to avoid reprinting accounts of weird experiences that have been prepared by unidentified informants; such accounts often omit significant information (such as where and when the event or its anticipation occurred), details that could, possibly, corroborate the story being related. Anonymous accounts read like folklore; possibly they are. If so, David Boyle was right to include them in this series of columns.

Are these accounts veridical? That is, are they truthful? We will never know for sure. No one will ever be able to prove the truth of them one way or the other. In the meantime, they make for delightful reading today.

Remarkable Dreams

(reported by David Boyle in *The Globe*)

A Toronto gentleman, who encloses his card, gives us two very remarkable instances of dream verification, for which he vouches.

"I notice," he says, "in Saturday's *Globe*, several accounts of strange dreams, etc., and with your permission will relate one that I think has never been related before, because the person who told it to me would not allow it to be made public, for fear that his friends would laugh at him. He is now dead, and while I reserve the right to keep his name out of print, I think the dream sufficiently interesting to chronicle.

"D'Arcy McGee was advertised to lecture some thirty odd years ago in the Music Hall, Toronto, and my relative, being a prominent man in connection with the Mechanics' Library, as it was then, and a prominent citizen, was taking a great deal of interest in the work, being at the hall almost every evening for a week. The night McGee was shot my friend wakened up about midnight, and sitting up in bed, wakened his wife, who asked if he were ill. 'No,' he responded, 'but I have had a very nasty dream. I thought I saw D'Arcy McGee shot.' His wife replied: 'You have been thinking so much of him lately it has naturally made you anxious and restless.' After some minutes they both went to sleep again. In the morning they were at breakfast when The Globe arrive, and almost the first thing they read was that D'Arcy McGee had been shot dead at Ottawa. Mr. ———— was so upset by this news and his dream that he was unwell for days. He made his wife promise never to tell the dream to anyone, but it was told to me years afterwards, as a great secret.

"Can any person explain this to me? The person who dreamed this dream was one of the best known men in Canada, and no one would doubt his word or that of his wife.

"Some six years ago a very dear friend and neighbour of mine was taken suddenly ill. He immediately sent for me. I found him in bed, with what was only a very severe cold. That night I dreamed he would die Thursday morning at three minutes to 3. So impressed with this dream was I that I told it to my wife in the morning. Tuesday night I sat up with him. Wednesday two other friends sat up, but I was there, too.

"About 11 p.m. the other two wanted me to go home and rest, telling me I could take their places on Thursday. I then told them of my dream, and said I would remain until 3 o'clock, and if my friend was alive then I would go home. He was resting all day and did not seem seriously ill. About 1 o'clock he took a turn for the worse, and died exactly at three minutes to 3, as I had dreamed."

MY FIGHT FOR LIFE WITH AN OCTOPUS

This gripping narrative appeared in the *Daily News* (Dawson, Yukon Territory) on November 28, 1902. The writer is identified as Lillan Ferguson, but the source of the story is effectively Captain S.F. Scott, so I have given the two men a joint byline here. It is really an "as told to" tale.

The tale is exciting, one that is not soon forgotten. Yet the reader is right if he thinks the contribution of Lillan (not Lillian!) Ferguson is somewhat overwrought!

My Fight for Life with an Octopus

(reported by Captain S.F. Scott & Lillan Ferguson in *The Daily News*)

Struggling to free himself from the deadly embrace of that ocean vampire, an octopus; fighting as frantic and unequal a battle as ever man fought on land or sea, his life blood crimsoning the chill salt waters that shrouded him while each agonizing instant hastened him toward a fate that would terrify the bravest and boldest; wounding his foe at last and triumphing over death in hideous guise — this was the peril and this the miracle which makes Captain S.F. Scott, mariner and miner, an exceptionally heroic figure.

Other men have fallen into the arms of devil fish, but they have not lived to tell the tale.

Captain Scott, indeed, does not tell his willingly.

He is trying to forget.

Two hours of incessant pain and terror, with one's body submerged, one's strength gradually giving way, one's limbs lacerated by a bloodthirst thing below, and no sign of succor across the green waste of waters, are not pleasant memories. But when a man has proved himself a marvel of physical endurance, when he can match his muscle against the might of such a monster as the octopus and vanquish it without a weapon and with both hands clinging to an overturned boat, the story may not be allowed to lapse untold. The plain tragic truth of it is far too interesting.

With five friends Captain Scott had gone out for a pleasure trip in a small yacht. The breeze died away and they set sail for port in a hatful of wind. Becalmed in a region that Captain Scott, who knew every trick of the currents there and the position of every rock, realized was dangerous, he decided to row in toward shore, select a safe spot for anchorage and signal his friends to bring on the yacht with their oars.

What happened within the next two hours makes a chapter of incident thrilling enough to have been found in the fanciful fiction of Victor Hugo, instead of being here set down, plain facts from the actual life experience of Captain S.F. Scott, the mariner who has turned from the terrors of the sea to delve for the treasures of the mainland.

On that Sunday morning, while the yacht lay

> As like as a painted ship
> Upon a painted ocean,

the captain pulled away from the craft with as little thought of pending danger as you or I would have in crossing a country road. A mile or so of rapid rowing and a school of whales, the blackfish species which frequent these waters, passed him. One of them struck the boat. It bounded like a cork into the air.

"What will the boys say?" he thought. It seemed such a joke to be upset by a whale.

But there was no more joking in store for him that day, nor for many days to come; nor for seven months to come — seven months of misery, when he did not know whether he would ever walk again.

Over in Victoria the good people present went from their worship to their homes. Miles away in the yacht the men smoked and talked, idling the time that must necessarily elapse before they could move shoreward. Now and then one of them glanced over the shoulder to see if the captain had signaled. Afar off something lay on the water that looked like a bunch of seaweed. How could they know that it was the head of their comrade in distress? That the eight arms of a maneater were all this time tightening around him, each a horny hook obeying its preying instinct to drag him to a feast on the ocean bed?

But the man in the water had not sailed the world over to die now. And he had not been an athlete all his life to vain purpose. His splendid strength and his unconquerable courage wrought the miracle that saved him.

Captain Scott is today in as fine physical condition as though he had not escaped from an encounter with an octopus which he is trying to forget. He is in this city on a business trip in connection with the United States–British Columbia Corporation, a mining company of which he is the vice president and general manager. He was born in St. John, New Brunswick; at thirteen, served under the Stars and Stripes, and at twenty-one was placed in command of a British ship. Exciting adventure in many forms has followed him throughout his career. He has been picked up four times at sea, once in the Pacific, west of Valparaiso, by the ship "Wonlock" of London; once by the ship "Edith Rose" of New York on a Christmas day off Cape Hatteras, where on a floating hulk he was rescued with a goat, a dog and a turtle; once by a Spanish man-of-war when the ship "Annie" burned off the isle of Cuba; and again on a Christmas day in a snow-storm, when he was shipwrecked on Wolf Rocks, off the Bay of Fundy, and a lighthouse keeper spied him on Flat Pot Rock, where for fifty-two hours he had been living on seaweed and snowballs. He was in Chile during the revolution and in the bombardment at Alexandria, when the ports were blockaded by the English fleet. Near Marseilles he put down a mutiny and saved the lives by losing a finger.

The Captain's Story

In September of last year, while in Victoria, British Columbia, I was installed by some friends to go for a sail in a small yacht. When he reached the vicinity of Race Rocks, about fifteen miles out from

Victoria, the wind suddenly died out, leaving the vessel in a dangerous position, owing to the fact that there was a very heavy current running between the various rocks thereabouts and Race Rock lighthouse.

Knowing the danger, I volunteered to go in a rowboat toward shore to find a suitable spot for anchorage. This was the best way out of our difficulty and could have been accomplished very easily had no misfortune occurred; but who could have foreseen that I was to fall into the clutches of a sea monster on the way? When a man has made the sea his home for a lifetime, surviving shipwreck and the worst that the elements can do to him, he is not looking for trouble in a becalmed sea within sight of land.

Lowering the yacht's small boat, I pulled toward the shore. I had arranged with my friends on board that I would put an oar on end as a signal that I had found anchorage, upon which they were to come directly after me, rowing the distance between us. When I got about a mile from the yacht and was using my two oars as rapidly as possible so that there should be no delay in our making safe anchorage, a school of blackfish passed me. Blackfish are in reality whales, their length being from thirty to fifty feet, the average fish being some forty feet long. It was a good-sized one that, unfortunately, shaped his course directly under my boat, striking it with such force that I was sent flying into the air, boat and all, while the oars shot beyond reach.

An old sailor doesn't mind a wetting; neither did the loss of oars bother me much, although they deprived me of my signals, for I could drift until my friends got concerned enough about me to come to the rescue. All this went through my mind when, coming to the surface after going down a considerable distance, I saw the boat a few feet off, upside down.

My hat was bobbing about near by, so I swam for it, then swam to the boat. I had just got my hands onto the keel to turn the boat over, when in the very instant of turning it I was seized like a flash around the legs, half way below the knees — seized with such tremendous strength and suddenness, at the same time pulled with such force downward that my hands still clutching the keel, the boat was jerked clean over and came down on the top of my head with a stinging blow.

Like lightning came the awful truth.

I was in the arms of a devil fish.

The waters in which I had been caught are known as the Juan de Fuca straits. The region swarms at times with the dreaded octopus. Once, when working a wreck there, the divers could not proceed until provided with knives, sharp and stout, to cut their way with. There is no mistaking the grasp of a devil fish. Every one of his eight powerful arms closes upon his prey like a vise and he pulls downward — down, down, until he reaches bottom and can uninterruptedly feed upon the veins of his victim.

The blow from the boat stunned me so far that I loosened my hold for an instant, then kicked and plunged so desperately that, to my joy, I succeeded in freeing myself from the creature below. But only for a few seconds.

Seizing the boat, I had just got her onto the keel and my arm under the thwart when the devil fish caught me again.

"Is this my end?" I thought, in despair. I realized the almost hopeless predicament that I was in, for what man might expect to escape from the clutches of an octopus? Had I sailed the world over to meet a fate like this at last? At least I would die hard. That devil should fight for his dinner.

It was a terrible battle for life. Although it must have lasted less than half an hour, it seemed interminable. The pain was excruciating, for every movement that I made in resistance lacerated my flesh and I began to grow weak from loss of blood. But I never relaxed my hold on the boat. I was in splendid physical condition at the time, and strength like that of a lion seemed to be given me. Four times I turned the boat over before I got her steady on her keel, for, with the devil fish pulling me and I trying frantically to kick myself free, I could not gauge my actions with any accuracy of judgment.

Finally, to my unspeakable relief, I felt the clutch on my legs loosen. I was free. I attribute this partly to my boots; they were unusually thick-soled, heavy calf, laced boots of English make, and must have injured the arms of the fish, compelling it to let go.

By this time the boat was full of water, her gunwales only about six inches above the surface and my head just out of water. I glanced in despair toward the yacht lying so tantalizingly near, yet so fatally far. I knew that my five comrades were lounging over there at ease, while I was suffering untold tortures both of body and of mind, expecting every instant to be seized by my old foe or a fresh one — perhaps as many others as could get their claws on my bleeding limbs. And all this while the men were wondering why "the captain" was so slow putting up that oar.

It was an hour and a half — it seemed like twenty years to me — before Mr. Berry, a New York man of the party, said: "What the deuce keeps the captain?" and spying the boat, exclaimed, "Boys, something's happened!" It was slow work, rowing the yacht up to me, and slow work getting me out of the cold water. I was chilled through and my clothing was a leaden weight in addition to my 225 pounds.

When I got aboard, where I was hauled by a rope, there were no dry clothes and no way of getting warm. A breeze sprang up dead ahead. It was then 1 o'clock of a Sunday morning, and we did not get into Victoria until 11 o'clock the next day. I went to bed at the hotel, and three weeks afterward was removed to the house of my brother-in-law. Seven weeks later I went to Seattle, where I had a relapse and was laid up in bandages again for eight weeks, unable to move as much as a toe. Finally, with the aid of canes, I managed to get to the train and went to the region of British Columbia where my mining interests are, and in that dry climate recovered thoroughly.

Altogether I was laid up for seven months as the result of my encounter with that beggar under water in the straits. My stomach was in such a condition from swallowing salt water that I had to live on milk for two months.

I went into the rowboat a bunch of iron. I came out of it a wreck. The skin was all gone from my flesh nearly to the knees, and above that it remained for weeks as black as a man's hat. But I'm back to my former weight and recently took a 270-mile horseback ride. I think a friend of mine hit it about right when he said to me the other day: "Gad, captain, they can't kill you unless they cut your head off."

THE WEIRD CREATURE

Here is a gripping news story about an oldish girl (or youngish woman) who is menaced by a witch (whom she initially mistakes for her own mother) at St. Margaret's Bay, Prince Edward Island.

Is it a tale of possession? A tale of delusion? A tale of domination? A tale of witchcraft? A tale of a witch doctor? The newspaperman who wrote the story was not really sure what it was, but he took delight in including a wealth of detail and in adding a happy ending, of sorts.

"Witchcraft Near Halifax" is reprinted from the *Herald* (Halifax, Nova Scotia), January 30, 1904. It is lightly copy-edited. It ends with references to Christian Scientists, homeopaths, and allopaths; they need no explanation because they are with us to this day. But John Alexander Downie (1847–1907) is a figure from the past. Around the turn of the last century the Scots-born preacher was known as the Healing Apostle. Downie established his own church in Chicago, Illinois, as well as a series of "healing homes." Public opinion turned against him when he founded his own authoritarian community called Zion in Illinois and declared himself to be the incarnation of the prophet Elijah. Apparently he had disciples in the Maritimes.

Witchcraft Near Halifax
Girl in St. Margaret's Bay Wrestled with Witch for Hours
Joe Weeno Drives the Evil Spirit Away with Cross of Dogwood
Doctor Called Afterwards Says Girl Had a Case of Hysteria

(from *The Herald*)

St. Margaret's Bay, January 28: — The spirit rapping lately reported from Prince Edward Island is altogether cast in the shade by a far more wonderful phenomenon, sensible and invisible, at a place known as The Puddle, on the north shore of St. Margaret's Bay.

A girl of about twenty, returning from a neighbour's house late at night, saw a woman sitting on the front door step of her home; the woman got up and walked towards the girl, who first supposed that this was her mother. The woman tried to persuade the girl to go away with her. After much spirit wrestling the girl got into the house; but still this witch, as the girl's parents claim it to have been, clung to the girl, who all night laboured hard to get rid of the weird creature that had possession of her. Next day, the girl's health no improving, or rather the witch not leaving her, a man from Lunenburg county, who happened to be in the neighbourhood, stated that he could drive the witch away. In addition to this power of divination he was accustomed to the use of hatchet and saw, so he got to work and made a cross of some rare wood and some small sticks of the same tree. These he carefully steeped in a decoction of mysterious liquids only known to this rare Alchemist himself. Asked as to its ingredients, the only reply that could among his many cabalistic terms be understood — and this he frequently repeated, was: "We no!" "We no!" This cross and the sticks, which fortunately were not of heavy material, were laid upon the poor girl's breast, together with several sharp knives, so arranged as it was positively stated, that the witch when leaving the girl would run into the blades and be killed forevermore, and the victim at once released from the wiles and wrestlings of the avid spirit. In addition to the above remedy a pig was killed and its heart, while yet warm, was stuck with nine ordinary pins; a fire was made, and when it reached a certain temperature known only to this wonderful "witchmaster," the pig's heart, still warm and studded with brass-headed pins, was thrown into the fire.

That this genius from the backwoods of Lunenburg county had some authority for his wonderful doings, let me quote from Shakespeare's Macbeth, Act IV, scene 1:

First Witch —
"Pour in sow's blood, that hath eaten
Her nine farrows; grease, that's sweaten
From the murderer's gibbet, thrown
Into the flame."

Doors were marked with crosses, switches used to chase or scare away the evil lady of the nether world. At one time the door of the room in which this bewitching maiden lay was kept tightly closed that the witch might not escape without being seen. Up to this time no one had yet seen it, but the father of the girl claims to have caught "it" and thrown "it" into the fire.

Neighbours far and near flocked to the house to witness the wonderful antics of the frail creature under the "spell," and to learn some facts pertaining to the strange affair. Some regretted that the shadow of old Salem and the seventeenth century still darken some minds of the twentieth; others thought the case an extremely complicated and mysterious one, while a few others felt certain that a witch had been caught in a snare. Eye witnesses state that the decoration and setting of knives on the girl's breast would have surpassed the adornments of a Red Indian brave. This professor of demonology and the jack-plane claims to have banished the witch that had done so much harm, and says what a fortunate thing he happened to be in the vicinity. Begone, you Christian Scientist! Move on, John Alexander Downie and your hosts! Get you gone you Homeopaths, and you black Allopaths, and make way for Joe Weeno, with his dogwood sticks steeped in extract of hemlock and his pig's heart pin cushion, for curing disease or driving ensnared witches into Hades.

Later, a doctor form an adjoining village has been called to see the girl, and states that it is a case of hysteria.

UGLY IDOL

One hundred years ago readers of daily newspapers expected to be entertained with weird and wonderful stories that passed as items of news. Come to think of it, the expectations of newspaper readers have remained pretty constant over the last century!

"Ugly Idol Startles an Ottawa Lady" appeared in the *Leader-Post* (Regina, Saskatchewan) on January 3, 1907. It certainly meets the need for weirdness. The contemporary reader would like to know more about poor Mrs. Tate, who had the fright of her life when she opened the glass box and beheld its frightful contents, and also about the background of "the former tenant"! And I find myself wondering whatever happened to the contents of the box.

Reading old newspaper columns and then transcribing them is not always a straight-forward procedure, especially given that the paper has disintegrated with the years and the researcher must work with microfiche, microfilm, and other forms of microprint. Hence lines of print, especially near folds and creases, or near edges of pages, are next to illegible when not altogether unreadable. This column presented a few problems of this sort, but I was lucky to be assisted by the researcher W. Ritchie Benedict, who supplied obscured lines. Like the Oriental object in the news story, mysteries linger!

Ugly Idol Startles an Ottawa Lady
Mrs. Tate Opens Glass Box Left by
Mysterious-looking Stranger and Gets Fright

(from *The Leader-Post*)

OTTAWA, Jan. 2:— A most remarkable little object, apparently half fish and half gorilla, was found yesterday evening by Mrs. R.C. Tate, 496 Rideau Street, under circumstances that almost rival some of the stories of Edgar Allan Poe. Certainly the supposed merman is one of the most hideously grotesque little things that can be imagined, and to run across it as Mrs. Tate did, in the dark garret, would disturb the nerves of the boldest.

One glance at the horrid Chinese idol, Hindu god, or whatever it is, and Mrs. Tate dropped it back into the glass box from which she had taken it and rushed down stairs in a condition bordering upon hysteria. Several of the neighbours rushed into the house upon hearing the cries, and it was some time before the ladies could look upon the savage semi-fish without a shudder. Stories were told of people in possession of such a replica of oriental religious value being mysteriously stricken down by unknown assassins, and Mrs. Tate refused to have the image in the house over night, remembering possibly the fantastic stories such as the "Moon-Stone" and other tales where idols' ears and images' eyes played most important roles in the deaths of whole families. As a solution in the matter, the peculiar object was taken to The Citizen office, where it now is, and may be seen by the morbidly curious. Just what the thing is supposed to represent is a mystery — in fact, more than one man has believed it to be a real merman, half ape and half shark. The story of the find is a most interesting and peculiar one.

About a foot long, the merman's lower half is fish, with fully developed tail, and six perfect fins. The upper part is certainly petrified, and a perfectly formed human or ape-like body. The hands are webbed with fierce-looking claws, while the big head, wrinkled and fearful, is turned to one side with a most malignant leer. Sharp teeth appear in the gums and the body is covered with long hairs. Altogether the effect is absolutely horrifying.

"A year ago in February," said Mrs. Tate, in telling the finding of the object, "a tall, dark-eyed man, with black hair, wearing a slouch hat and long grey coat, came to the front door and handed in a long glass box, hermetically sealed and apparently filled with wood. 'Give this to the man who used to live here,' the stranger said, smiling. 'He will know what I mean.'" The box was taken in and put in the hall for a week. No one called for it, and the garret was finally its resting place, where it lay for almost a year.

During Christmas week, Mrs. Tate made a lot of passe-partout work, and yesterday decided to make one more for a friend, overlooked at Christmas. No glass was to be had, and the lady was in despair until she thought of the glass box upstairs, left by the stranger a year ago. A little trouble brought the box to light, now covered with cobwebs, but hermetically sealed as first seen.

Taking a knife, the six glass sides were removed, when a black, cloth-covered board was found, with something fastened to it, and wrapped in yards and yards of wool. The last fold was torn away and the frightful little grinning merman was seen in the dim light of the attic. Uttering a shriek, Mrs. Tate rushed down-stairs and the house was in an uproar in a moment.

Why the strange man left the object for the former tenant, whose person left her recently, Mrs. Tate does not know; why the former tenant failed to call for his oriental idol, or whatever it is — all these points are a mystery.

PREMONITION OF DEATH

"The woods are full of creepy things…"

These are the opening words of a haunting children's song. There are indeed "creepy things" that haunt the woods, and there are chilling events and experiences that are creepy as well. The backwoods and farms are full of these, too.

Premonitions, predictions, prophecies, apprehensions, anticipations, presages, harbingers, signs, forerunners, warnings — whether in the guise of dream or vision — are events and experiences that have an eerie cast to them.

Or at least the reports of them are eerie.

There is no way to prove that a premonition has actually occurred, short of some impeachable record-keeping. This seldom pertains. Yet there is no substantial reason to doubt that premonitions do occur. They are certainly reported often enough. As long as the witnesses are reliable men and women with reputations as serious citizens to uphold, who have nothing at all to gain from an admission of "sensitivity" or "receptivity," then the report could be taken at face value.

In any case, all we have is the report. No one conducted an inquiry. Even if someone had sleuthed around, it is doubtful that much could be established, other than the word of the informant that events occurred as described.

"Mysterious Ethereal Agency Tells Father of His Son's Death" appeared in the *Lethbridge Herald* (Alberta) on December 15, 1930. The title is a little odd, as the news story, which is largely in the first person, make no reference to "ether" or any other medium or mechanism that might account for the creepy experience of Joseph Barrie.

Mysterious Ethereal Agency
Tells Father of His Son's Death

Premonition of Evil Leads Farmer to Confirmation of Fear

(Special to *The Herald*, Copyright 1930)

ARNPRIOR, DEC. 15:— Joseph Barrie, whose home is situated about 15 miles from Arnprior, in the Ottawa Valley, claims that on the night before his son was mysteriously shot to death, he had convincing assurance through strange channels that there was some kind of very serious trouble in his son's home, or in some manner having to do with his son. He was in a hunting lodge in the heart of the forest at the time; the hour was shortly after midnight, and so positive was he of impending danger to his son that he left the camp at break of day and proceeded directly to the home of his son. The body of the young man was hardly cold when he arrived.

This was not the first time Mr. Barrie has had such a premonition, he experienced it several times and on every occasion the strange warning was, unfortunately, well founded. He is one of the best-known farmers in McNab township, 67 years of age, a gentleman of integrity who is highly esteemed in the community in which he lives and he related the following strange story:

"About a week ago, I left my home for a hunting camp on the shores of White lake and shortly before I went away I visited the home of my son, Warner, inspecting with him his substantial farm buildings. All was well.

"I retired early on Sunday night in camp with the intention of rising at daybreak fore the morning chase. I ate nothing after partaking of the evening meal about 6 o'clock. I fell asleep quickly enough, but shortly after midnight I sat bolt upright in bed, convinced that I had heard the report of a gun shot and that in some way my son Warner was involved in serious trouble. I had premonitions of the kind on other occasions, when my worst fears had been realized, and it was with difficulty I again settled down to rest.

Fears Are Confirmed

"Every time I slumbered I had a feeling that Warner was calling and, finally, the mysterious suggestions became so clearly defined, that I rose, partially dressed, lit the lamp, and paced the floor. The sighing of the wind in the tall pines and the impenetrable darkness outside gave the surroundings an eerie appearance and I waited impatiently for the first glimpse of dawn that I might start on the long, tedious journey homeward. The call was impelling and nothing could detain me.

"About 4 o'clock I was on my way not to my own home, which was considerably closer, but to the home of my son, arriving there toward noon. I had spoken to no one on the way, yet when I reached the door of the house I hesitated: I lacked the courage to go in, thoroughly convinced that something terrible had happened. I then did the unusual thing. I knocked. My son's young wife opened the door; her countenance and swollen eyes convinced me that my worst fears were realized, that the premonition, or second-sight, or dream, or whatever you prefer to call it, was correct — Warner was found in a pool of blood on the floor of the stable where he had gone, as was his custom every morning, to tend the horses. He had risen as usual, made a fire in the kitchen stove, went out of the door whistling, never to return."

Asked if he really had experiences of this kind before, Mr. Barrie, without hesitation, replied that he had. This statement was corroborated by his wife standing close by, a lovable old lady with snow-white hair and large blue eyes that were filled with tears.

"When our son, Lawrence, died in Saskatchewan, my husband had the same experience," she said. "On awakening in the morning he told me was afraid some serious trouble had befallen the boy. So convinced were we that, although we had received no information from him, we were debating whether his father should hasten westward to be with him when a telegram arrived announcing that the poor boy had died early that morning following an operation."

The sweet-faced old mother brushed away a fear with the corner of her apron.

Further questions elicited from Mr. Barrie the fact that his father possessed this strange faculty of sensing disaster to those close to him. Asked if he were not liable to confuse a dream with premonition of evil, he said the latter is, to him, much more clearly defined in detail, much more insistent and impelling than a dream.

"CADDY" THE SEA SERPENT

We like to think of our forebears as being credulous about ghosts and spirits, and especially uncritical about the existence of sea serpents and lake monsters.

Truth to tell, our predecessors were no more gullible than we are today — though that is saying a lot. Judging by our supermarket tabloids, we are a mindless lot!

Cryptozoology is the study of hidden or strange creatures. It is a subject that may be taken with a grain of salt — and some laughing gas. Cryptozoologists, who range from naive enthusiasts to experienced scientists, have studied reports and sightings of "Caddy," the nickname of Cadborosaurus, the sea serpent frequently described as cavorting in the waters of Cadboro Bay off the coast of Victoria, British Columbia. But so far no cryptozoologist worth his salt has ever reported having a conversation with the serpent.

What the cryptozoologist may fear to report is grist for the mill of newspapermen. "'Caddy' the Sea Serpent Tells Why [It] Came Back" comes from *The Dawson News* (Dawson, Yukon Territory), May 1, 1934. The story is amusing, for it turns the tables on the newspaperman and the reader, and in upsetting expectations, it recalls "The Canterville Ghost," Oscar Wilde's classic ghost story about a courteous old English ghost that is frightened to the point of death by an American family with bratty children!

I tried to trace the little verse that is quoted — about taking power who can — but have yet to find the source of it.

"Caddy" the Sea Serpent
Tells Why It Came Back

(from *The Dawson News*)

From the middle eye of "Caddy" the Victoria sea serpent a tear ran down off his forelock and he brushed it away gently with his right dorsal fin.

"So you do believe in me?" he said.

"Certainly," said the newspaper man. "Why shouldn't I?"

"Caddy" shook his head. "The incorrigible sceptism of the human race," he said. "Think of what Christopher Columbus endured before he met Ferdinand and Isabella. Think of what they did to Robert Fulton until he succeeded in sailing his steamboat up the Hudson. Think of Galileo. When I made my appearance in Victoria recently it was the same old harsh world that I encountered. The newspapers commented upon my appearance as extravagant nonsense."

The sea serpent stared straight ahead of him, her or it.

"Do you know," he said, "I almost didn't show up at all. I had, to put quite plainly, grown sick of the same weary round, millenniums and eons since I was born in the primeval slime. To what purpose this recurrent parade in the public eye — in 1817, and in 1839, and in 1859, and in 1875, and in 1897, and so on? Like a tiresome Business Cycle."

"Why, sure," said the reporter. "There was a picture of you in the papers the other day as seen by a navigating officer in the Caribbean, all dips and curves. You looked exactly like the monthly carloadings from December, 1928 to February, 1934, inclusive. But pardon me, you were saying —"

"I was saying," said the sea serpent, "that I grew tired of it all. People were fast ceasing to believe in me and I was beginning to lose credence in myself. After all, one was so dreadfully old, so out of place in a modern world. My time was past, I belonged in the ooze of the Eocene, not in the full blaze of twentieth century civilization. And then all at once it came to me suddenly one night how foolish and blind I was.

"I remember the moment distinctly," continued the Monster. "I was then swimming off Tasmania, Gibraltar, the south shore of Lake Erie, off the coast of Vancouver Island and within sight of the bathers on Waikiki Beach. In the excitement of the new revelation I remember standing upright in the water, trumpeting shrilly through my trunk and flapping my wings exultantly. For the thought had come to me that I was not obsolete even if I was very old. I recalled all at once that fashions had changed. Ever so many old things were coming back."

"For instance?" said the reporter.

"Well," said the Sea Serpent, "I looked out on the world and saw men reviving so many customs, practices and beliefs from the past — all the way back from the centuries, from the jungle, from the primeval slime. Here was somebody trying to get back to Robespierre. Here was somebody else trying to get back to the Roman Empire. Here was somebody else getting back the ethics of the primitive Teutonic forests. And on every hand were clubbings and shootings and hangings and decapitations. Neighbours were being taught or compelled to hate each other. Children were taught to laugh at notions like human brotherhood and human freedom, and instead were drilled in gas masks and hand grenades. They were made to recite as a creed:

> The good old plan,
> That he shall take who has the power
> And he shall keep who can.

"Well," said the Sea Serpent, "so I looked around and said to myself, 'Heck,' I said to myself, 'I am not out of date after all. I belong. I fit in.' I said to myself, 'With so many monstrous things about, why not a Sea Monster?' And here I am."

CURSE OF THE DEVIL WOMAN

I wish I knew the identity of Roy Cooper. He sounds like an interesting man.

Cooper is the writer of the following article, which was originally published in the *Winnipeg Free Press*, December 29, 1962. I learned that he was never an employee of the newspaper, but he was a freelance contributor of articles on popular history to its Saturday edition.

It is too bad he was not more specific about the location of the Indian reserve as well as the identities of the Cree people he mentions. I am also curious about the devil woman, and am sorry the article was not illustrated. Magazine illustrators and Hollywood casting directors would know what to make of her appearance!

Forty years after the events described it would be difficult if not impossible to substantiate the story told here. Yet in general terms the account is consistent with tales of curses and cures of a supernatural nature told by the Native peoples as well as the pioneers and settlers in the backwoods of the country one century or more ago.

Curse of the Devil Woman

(reported by Roy Cooper in *The Winnipeg Free Press*)

In 1961 a strange event occurred on an Indian reserve in northern Manitoba. A boy of seventeen was suddenly and without warning stricken with disfigurement — his face was twisted badly out of shape on the right side.

This caused great alarm among the Indians. It was, they said, the work of a devil woman. My interest was aroused, and I set out to get all the information that I could. This I felt was something out of the past.

The first thing was to speak to the boy's father, but before I had time to leave the house, the father burst in. His face had a look of terror. He begged me to help him and his boy. He spoke half in Cree and half in English, and it took me several minutes to calm him down enough for me to understand him.

"Don's face worse. Very bad," he sobbed. I advised the natural thing.

"Get him to hospital right away," I said.

"No good do that," he replied. "Doctors not help him. This happen before the doctor not help him."

At this, I tried to assure him that this was purely a natural sickness. Probably the boy had a cold in his face.

"No, no, no!" he cried. "Devil woman do this before. You white men, you know nothing about these things."

I tried for half an hour to get him to let me send his son into the hospital.

"No, doctors not help my boy. I fetch medicine men to reserve." Nothing I could do or say would make him change his mind.

During the next couple of days, two medicine men did arrive on the reserve and I questioned a number of Indians about them.

They spoke of the medicine men with awe and I could see plainly that even now, in this day and age, they feared them. Several Indians told me that I would find the church empty on Sunday if the medicine men were still on the reserve. They were still there the following Sunday and the church was next to being empty.

The medicine men had stayed on because another Indian had been stricken. This time it was a woman in her fifties, and the left side of her face had been affected. The medicine men had visited the boy and after much chanting had dressed the boy's face with herbs, leaving instructions that he must not go out for a certain number of days and that no one was to visit him during this time.

His brothers and sisters had to leave the house and at the end of this period he would be completely cured. The medicine men also visited the woman, giving the same treatment and instructions.

Several days had gone by after the medicine men left the reserve, when suddenly the Indian woman sent for me. I went to see her, and found her very frightened. She told me she was not getting any better, and I advised her to go to the doctor right way.

On returning she told me that the doctor could not help her. "He told me I was too late in coming to him," she said, "and that he could do nothing for me." The Indians said she would not get better because she had not done as the medicine men had ordered. The boy followed the instructions to the letter and completely recovered. The woman to this day still has a partial disfigurement.

The boy's father said that the medicine men had told him who had caused the twisted faces, and why. The person responsible was an Indian woman whose mother had been very active in this kind of thing before.

The boy had been stricken the medicine men said because this woman believed him to be responsible for her daughter's pregnancy. I know that the daughter was expecting a child. It turned out later, however, that the boy was innocent of the charge. The cause of the woman being stricken was also given by the medicine men. It was, they said, because the two women were bitter enemies.

Something I cannot explain is that the woman they label "devil woman" stayed behind the locked door of her house weeping from the time the medicine men set foot on the reserve until they left.

Was this disfigurement from natural causes? Or was it in fact, as the Indians believe, the work of a devil woman?

Although there are many similar cases on record I believe these two were victims of natural causes. The medicine men were able to bring about a cure because of the absolute faith of their patient. I must admit however, that when I hear the many strange tales the Indians tell, I find myself wondering.

PERSONAL ACCOUNTS

THE GHOST OF MARY MOWAT

The following story was posted to the newsgroup *Alt.folklore.ghost-stories* on the Internet on June 7, 1994, at 02:38:31 GMT. (Internet posting times are very precise!)

The Ghost of Mary Mowat

David Sztybel

I would now like to post a ghost story that I was told by a friend, who experienced the haunting in question.

My friend, like me, is a university student pursuing philosophy, and she lives a couple of hours away from me by train. She seemed completely sincere in telling me this, and her account was corroborated by her father, mother, and one of her friends who also encountered an unaccountable presence in the midst of this haunting. The setting is in London, Ontario, a small city in the southern part of the province. Here is the story itself, with my friend's name changed in order to protect the privacy of her and her family.

Cat Robertson is the name of my friend. Her father is a manager of a local grocery store, and came to befriend a client of the store, Mrs. Mowat. As Mr. Robertson was a kindly fellow, he assisted Mary Mowat on occasion when she needed it. The woman was elderly and was living with a sister who was older. When the sister passed on, Mary came to depend more and more on Mr. Robertson. She felt alone in the world without him, as she was otherwise bereft of family, at least in that part of the world. As time wore on, Mary fell ill. Gravely ill. Mr. Robertson was at her deathbed, and she specifically instructed him that she had left her old house to him and his family in her will, and the Robertson family was to live there after Mary's death. Mr. Robertson agreed.

Mary died, and an inspection of an old grandfather clock in Mary's home revealed that the hand stopped at exactly the time of the woman's death. This was remarked to be odd, but nothing much was made of it at the time.

As things developed, Mary's old home went uninhabited. As later events unfolded, however, it became evident that where the Robertsons were living was not to be inhabited by them alone. Several incidents, suggestive of a full-scale haunting, lead me to believe that the Robertsons themselves were haunted by the spirit of Mary Mowat. Haunting of persons is much less common, supposedly, than haunting of dwellings, but this appeared to be just such a rare case.

My friend Cat was almost in her mid-teens at the time, and remembers being terrified of being alone in the house. She would be in her room, and hear footsteps out in the hall, and finally a knocking at her door when she knew that no one was home. She would hide in the closet in terror until her family came back home. Others in the family could hear the sound of voices coming from other rooms, as though a television set were playing on a low volume setting. The words were not quite audible. Whenever a Robertson would go into the room from whence the sound seemed to emanate, however, silence would ensue.

Not all the strange sounds were unaccompanied by other strange phenomena. A heaving and rumbling from the basement prompted one of the braver Robertsons to rush down to the basement, where the sound seemed to come from. Arriving in the laundry area, the Robertson was astonished to see that the washing machine was now in the middle of the laundry room, whereas it had not been before. It would seem that the rumbling sound was the machine being moved, by some unknown entity, across the floor.

And the movement of objects did not end there. Cat's boyfriend at the time, call him Fritz, appeared to be an object of displeasure for the spirit. One time when he was visiting Cat, a nearby chair was seen by many to be flung through the air at him, hitting him. Objects from a basement room were found upstairs, although no one had moved them.

Such occurred even when this room was locked. Perhaps the most astonishing transubstantiation was observed when an object, which someone lost while touring eastern Canada, appeared in the Robertsons' midst. They were bewildered. But it did not end there.

Some friends of Cat, against her wishes, conducted a sitting with a Ouija board, in order to determine what was behind these strange occurrences. The board became active, it seemed, but the message received did not seem to make sense. The participants (Cat was not among them) asked who was present (besides the living). The board said: MMVMOM.

Only later did Cat and her family realize that this represented the initials of the dead woman's family: Mary Mowat, Violet Mowat, and Oliver Mowat. The last two named were Mary's older sister, and younger brother, who perished in the ditches of World War One.

Many of the ghostly effects that the Robertsons experienced were downright eerie. A statue of a blacksmith, a likeness of a man who inhabited the site of Mary's home early in the century, when that part of London was still young and rural, was among the objects inherited from Mary Mowat. Its eyes once glowed red. Cat's brother claimed he saw slime dripping down a mirror, and then disappear when he did a double-take. The mother of the family recalls napping in her room, lying on the bed, and hearing someone open the door, enter the room, and then lie down beside her. She assumed it was her husband. Mrs. Robertson rolled over and opened her eyes. She screamed. It was a corpse that she saw lying beside her.

One day, Mrs. Robertson, the only one ever to see a spectre, saw an apparition of Mrs. Mowat while in the upstairs hallway. The ghost was standing at the top of the stairs, gazing towards the front door. Finally, the Robertsons did move into the Mowat residence, and that was all.

A HOUSE NEAR PEGGY'S COVE

Some of the most exciting material on the Internet is to be found in the newsgroup called *Alt.folklore.ghost-stories*. It is maintained by a person who identifies himself (or herself) as Obiwan. (The name recalls the wise warrior Obiwan "Ben" Kenobi of *Star Wars* fame.) On May 6, 1995, I came up with "The Futon Ghost." The posting bears the signature "Richard."

A House Near Peggy's Cove

"Richard"

This account is similar to the experience that I had about two years ago.

My brother had just bought a house near Peggy's Cove in Nova Scotia, and I decided to head east, congratulate my brother on his first home purchase, and give myself a month's vacation on the East Coast. Considering that the house had just been bought and my brother and sister-in-law had not fully furnished the house, I found myself sleeping on a large futon on the floor of a rather bare bedroom.

For the first two weeks I slept like rock. However, one night while I was drifting off to sleep, I felt a faint "fluttering" just under my right eye. Believing that it was a moth or June Bug, I quickly brushed it away with my hand, but I felt nothing. I concluded it must have been a moth of some sort.

The next night I was "visited" once more. Again, I was drifting off to sleep when I heard something rather heavy being placed on the pillow beside me. Being so close to the floor, my first thought was that a rat had crawled up onto the futon and was slowly making its way towards my head. Not being too fond of rodents, I quickly sat up, and just before pushing myself off the futon, I felt something touch me just under my right eye! I nearly jumped out of my skin! I switched on the light, but nothing was there.

The next morning, I told my brother and sister-in-law of my experience, and as to be expected, they were skeptical. To be truthful, several months after that night I started having doubts as well — maybe it was just a dream. However, something else happened in that room that re-enforced my belief in my experience.

Exactly a year after my visit, a friend of the family was sleeping in the same room and on the same futon. Supposedly, when she was drifting off to sleep, she heard the sheets moving and felt someone slide into bed beside her. She screamed, and the experience ended. Later she concluded that it — the ghost — must have been the size of a child. This was due to where it was in contact with her body.

I can't say that I believe without a doubt that ghosts do exist, but I now have an "open mind" on the subject.

A HAUNTED HOUSE IN PRESCOTT

Readers who are familiar with the Internet and with e-mail will know
that it is possible to join a newsgroup and be sent letters or postings
about subjects of interest. Each day, at no cost, a kind-hearted person
who calls himself Obiwan selects and sends a new, true-life ghost story
to me and to other like-minded Internet subscribers. Here is one such
message from James F. Robinson. It has been nominally edited. It was
received on June 15, 1995.

A Haunted House in Prescott

James F. Robinson

I think it is about time that I contributed a story. This is it!

I grew up in a haunted house in Prescott, Ontario. My father had
bought an old carriage barn that had been behind a funeral parlour. A
great aunt of ours had died in it of a heart attack when the coffin of her
late husband fell off the wagon, broke open, and his body sat up in
reflex. They say that a deranged man hanged himself in the rafters of
the same barn.

My father moved the barn to a triple lot down the street and placed
it on a foundation. He stripped the planks off and built a spacious,
three-bedroom home around the shell of the squared timbers and whatever else lived there. After we moved in, we began to experience some
strange happenings. There was a closet in the east bedroom that would
not stay locked. Back then we had the old latch-key locks. We would
lock the closet door in the evening and then sit back and watch. At
about midnight, the key would turn by itself, unlocking the door. Then

the door would swing open. It got to the point where we simply left the door unlocked and open. My sister, who slept in the room for a while, would wake up screaming, claiming to see a man hovering over her, showing only from the waist up and having hangman's noose around his neck. The apparition appeared to be trying to choke her. Dad moved us boys in. We never saw the ghost, but both of us would occasionally wake up with constricted throats.

My sister, who appeared to be psychic, also saw our dead great aunt, who would rush down the hall. If you were in the hall, you would feel a cold rush of wind. Auntie would then pass through the bedroom door and scare off the ghost with the noose.

Jim & Maureen, Vancouver, B.C.

Response

Stories on the Internet often generate responses. Here is a response to "A Haunted House in Prescott."

Great story, Jim.

Good thing the great-aunt kept an eye out for the family.

The story regarding the circumstances of her death reminds me of a story my Dad told me. Mind you he told us this story when we were kids.

This story will throw everyone for a loop…

I don't remember if he witnessed it or a relative of his did, but nonetheless, he and mom are visiting me this weekend, and I'll find a way to pop this question "out of the blue."

Anyway, apparently my family was tending to my granddad's funeral, mind you, this is Mexico a long, long time ago. The family was poor and usually the funerals were held at the home. Well, it seems that this granddad was laid out on the table. (He died due to heart problems.) Just envision all these people praying, crying, etc., at the house when … BE WARNED THE NEXT PARAGRAPH YOU READ WILL BE GRAPHIC AND VERY GROSS: Apparently, the late granddad sits up (in reflex?), looks around (while people are screaming in panic and just being scared witless), vomits, and collapses on the table again, "dead." =:-O!

Long time after everyone calmed down, ol' granddad was promptly buried. And to the best of my guess, last rites administered, again.

Angie :)

LA VIEILLE CHAPELLE RAMSAY

John Robert Colombo

La Vieille Chapelle Ramsay, or the Old Ramsay Chapel, is a guest house with a picturesque situation on the south side of the Chemin des Pères. From its promontory the visitor overlooks the city of Magog in the distance, as it stretches along the eastern shores of Lake Memphrémagog in Quebec's Eastern Townships. The lake itself is said to be the habitat of a fabulous lake monster known as Memphré. Further along the road lies the Benedictine abbey, St-Benoît-du-Lac. Between the chapel and the abbey is a roadway that takes one to the summer home of the late novelist Mordecai Richler. (Odd to have him living between these two religious sites!) The location of the Old Ramsay Chapel is not only picturesque, it is inspired.

The guest house is a bed and breakfast establishment with an art gallery and shop to display local arts and crafts. The establishment is owned and operated by a charming couple, Regina Makuch and Jean-Louis Le Cavalier, and their one child. Regina was born in the Maritimes and is of Ukrainian and Celtic background. Jean-Louis is a Quebecker from Mont-Saint-Hilaire to the north. They are friendly and handy and well-suited to the operation of La Vieille Chapelle Ramsay.

The seventeen-room Ramsay mansion with chapel dates from the 1860–80 period. When Regina and Jean-Louis first saw it, they realized it was an ideal house for their use and that it could be readily restored and converted into a guest house. It was only after they had acquired it that they learned that the Monseigneur David Shaw Ramsay had built it as his residence.

Some reference books lend a hyphen to his name. David Shaw Ramsay (or David Shaw-Ramsay) was born in Scotland. Ramsay

(1827–1906) was a Presbyterian cleric who settled in Quebec, where in 1859 he converted to Catholicism. He was received into the Jesuit order in England in 1867. He returned to Quebec and was appointed chaplain of the Montreal Prison in 1891. Six years later he became a parish priest in the Magog area, taking up full-time residence in the mansion. He died in Montreal; his remains are interred in the Cathedral of Montreal.

The main characteristic of his residence outside Magog is the large, second-storey chapel with its high ceiling. The Monseigneur caused it to be built, and here he conducted both private and parish services.

The following event occurred in November 1994. Regina Makuch and Jean-Louis Le Cavalier, on the market for a house to convert to bed-and-breakfast use, were immediately attracted to the possibilities of the Ramsay mansion, but they knew nothing of its history.

Regina regards herself as a sensitive person, someone who picks up feelings, thoughts, and ambiences. In the house she felt she could hear voices. More a feeling than a sound, she sensed one voice in particular, one sound more than all the others. It was a sobbing sound. She delved into the history of the house. When she learned about the Monseigneur, she felt he was attempting to communicate with her. A short while later she experienced visions, seeing the Monseigneur's face, sensing that he wanted his chapel restored as a place for Christians to pray and meditate, where people could find answers to their questions. The voices and the vision stressed that the work of restoration should begin in earnest, and that once the chapel was restored, people would flock there. Work on the chapel commenced, and the three guest rooms were completed on January 12, 1995, when La Vieille Chapelle Ramsay was formally opened. Since then business has been brisk.

Each of the three guest rooms has its own motif: dolphins, doves, deer. The lounge includes a snowy owl in flight. Akella, the wolf, dominates the hallway. The wall murals are the work of the artist Geneviève Reesör.

The walls of the chapel, the focal point of the residence, were freshly plastered and the wood was reworked. Local artist Erik Léo Trudel was commissioned to decorate the vaulting room, painting the walls and ceiling sky blue and adding baroque figures, including the black-robed Monseigneur holding a happy baby in his arms and a baroque orchestra of cute angels. One angel, who is strumming the harp, has Regina's face; another angel is recognizably Jean-Louis. An art historian might describe the work as *faux*-folk, rather in the manner of artist Louis de Niverville. The chapel is most intriguing and inviting: peasant baroque.

The uniqueness of the Old Ramsay Chapel is a testimony to the hard work of Regina and Jean-Louis, as well as to the power of vision.

I made the notes that appear here on Friday, July 14, 1995, after staying overnight, viewing the chapel, and conducting an interview with Regina Makuch.

La Vieille Chapelle Ramsay is located a ninety-minute drive south from Montreal; along Autoroute 10, Exit 115-S, follow Highway 112, take Chemin des Pères in the direction of St-Benoît-du-Lac for 4.6 kilometres.

I am informed that ownership of the Chapelle has since changed hands but that the murals remain a testimonial to the vision of Regina and the devotion of Jean-Louis. Perhaps I should also acknowledge the spirit of the Monseigneur.

THE HAUNTED DUPLEX

This one is a ghost story set in an unspecified community in Saskatchewan.

It comes from a correspondent who identifies himself or herself as "Lizard." It originally appeared on the newsgroup *Alt.folklore.ghost-stories* on July 19, 1995.

The Haunted Duplex

"Lizard"

Across the street from the fair grounds is a row of older housing authority duplexes. They are all somewhat run down, and the population in the area consists mainly of recently unemployed or unemployable persons. One of these units, on the east side of the second building from the corner, had been re-rented sixteen times in the space of two years, often by people who moved away to identical units in the same row. A friend of mine was hired to clean this unit and re-do the kitchen floor, so he brought along his usual staff of 3 people in addition to himself to do this.

When they arrived, things seemed normal enough. All of the surrounding units were empty and waiting to be refurbished in the same manner as this particular one, so it was very quiet. The bathroom upstairs needed some serious help, so my friend went upstairs with the other two men to see to it, while the woman they had brought along to help worked in the kitchen.

While washing the floor, she moved aside the stove and under it was a bloodstain. It looked as fresh and new as if it had just been spilled. She tried to scrub it off, but every time she succeeded, she'd turn her back while the water was drying and it would re-appear. After three times doing this, she started to get freaked out and called the men to come down. They all agreed that it was strange, so they ripped up the linoleum.

This solved the problem … for about twenty minutes. Blood started to ooze from the floorboards, looking "half-congealed." She couldn't believe it. She yelled for the men to come down again, and they did. They agreed to go home and try again the next day, saying it was probably a dead or dying cat or dog.

The next day, they returned. The bloodstain was on the floorboards, so they decided to re-cover the floor. This took the morning, but when they were done, the floor, one solid piece of linoleum, looked as shiny and new as a show home. Satisfied, they returned to cleaning the upstairs.

After about fifteen minutes, the woman in the kitchen dared to look at the floor again. It was back, but that wasn't all … that section of the linoleum had somehow reverted to the dingy, grey, dirt-encrusted look of the previous lino.

She dropped the bucket she was holding and tried to scrub it clean. Of course, it didn't work. But, as she was scrubbing, the sobbing and screams of a young boy made themselves heard. The men upstairs heard them too, and came rushing down the stairs. They found the woman fainted on the kitchen floor, so one of them stayed with her while the others went to find the source of the cries. The sound didn't exist outside, or in the adjoining or surrounding duplexes. Only in that one.

They quickly gathered their gear together and left. My friend dropped off his workers at their homes, then went to talk to the people at the housing authority.

It turned out that that unit, which had been built in 1936, had been occupied during the 60s by a young single mother and her eight-year-old son. They lived relatively quietly until the boy's father came by one day to see him. The father had an argument with the mother, and a struggle ensued. In the mêlée, the father's gun went off, killing the boy. Both parents ran, not wanting to be charged with murder or manslaughter, leaving the boy to bleed to death alone on the kitchen floor.

The linoleum has been changed in the duplex twelve times since that happened, but the blood always comes back. None of the tenants who have lived there since have stayed longer than a month, some of them preferring to live on the street.

Well, there's the end. My friend only went back once, just to see. The last renovations included two layers of lino. It hasn't helped.

NO ONE WANTED TO SLEEP IN THE ROOM

I found this story on the Internet on November 6, 1995, and communicated with its author, who kindly gave me permission to reproduce it here. Ron Sandler posted it to the moderator of the newsgroup called "X Archives."

The story is a good instance of the kind of haunting that has a history and is a happening. In the case of most hauntings, an uncommon event took place in the past, usually one the participants today had no knowledge of, that continues to influence the present in a manner that seems to be plausible, though improbable, if not impossible. In this instance the haunting is the "anniversary" of the historical event, the reverberation or echo of the past event into the corridors of the present.

There are many stories like this one in the "X Archives." Its Internet address is *http://www.crown.net/X/Stories/TDRoom.html.*

No One Wanted to Sleep in the Room

Ron Sandler

I've told this one several times, and it is true. It is partially folklore, and partially a personal experience for I have witnessed the paranormal phenomena. So here it is.

Amherstburg, Ontario, is a lovely, sleepy, old community on the Detroit River. It is an hour away from a large metropolitan area, and it still seems to be caught in an era from a previous century.

One of my best friends at the time, Patti H., still lived with her parents while she was attending the University of Windsor. Her parents bought an old, turn-of-the-century farm house with a store-front to house her father's jewelry shop. Patti owned two very large sheep dogs, and the move to a large house in the country was welcomed by all of them.

At first, the phenomenon was viewed as an annoyance. There was a back bedroom that was always cold. No matter an addition space heater was added, the room remained bone-chilling cold.

Then, Patti noticed that neither one of her sheep dogs would enter the room. When forced, they would growl, put their ears back, and leave as soon as allowed.

I was over, once, for dinner, and they asked me, without explaining why, to enter the bedroom and tell me what I thought of the room. (I had been part of a psychic experiment at Wayne State University in Detroit, and had been considered somewhat sensitive. I am an identical twin with an empathic link to my twin and have experienced visions on occasion.) I obliged them, and was "on edge" after I entered the room. I was chilled, and felt sad. I reported this to Patti, and she responded that was how they *all* felt about the bedroom. No one wanted to sleep in the room, or if they did, they had nightmares of a terrifying death.

Coupled with that, Patty reported that the bedroom door wouldn't stay closed but that it wouldn't drift open. The door would slam open with a bang on occasion, when no one was around it, and the windows were closed.

Sparked by curiosity, we contacted the local historical society and found out that a woman had been brutally murdered, knifed to death by her jealous husband, in that room, before he cut his own wrists and bled to death on the floor!

Needless to say, after that, if the dogs didn't want to go into that bedroom, they didn't have to.

The room is now being used for storage.

I HOPE YOU ENJOYED THESE

This item came via e-mail, in response to my request for information on ghosts in the vicinity of Guelph, Ontario. It was sent to me by Michael (whose last name I have withheld on request), who has been busy collecting ghost stories set in the Royal City, specifically those that are set on the picturesque campus of the University of Guelph.

I Hope You Enjoyed These

"Michael"

On Sat., 6 Jan. 1996, John Robert Colombo wrote:

I caught your request for ghost stories from Ontario's Royal City. As it happens, I'm currently looking for stories of hauntings, etc., for a publication to be called something like "Guidebook to Mysterious Sites in Ontario," so I could use any help I can get. I offer to swap what I have with you. I have a couple of stories from the Guelph area in my current book "Ghost Stories of Ontario" published by Hounslow Press (a division of Dundurn Press).

Dear Mr. Colombo:

I was pleased to hear from you. I have read a few of your books and found them very interesting. I enjoy books that place an emphasis on Canada and the paranormal.

Two books I have recently read that you might find of interest if you haven't already read them are *Ghost Stories of Saskatchewan* and *Ghost Stories of Prince Edward Island*. Unfortunately I don't remember the authors' names (I'm at work right now) and the P.E.I. one was only available on the Island.

Anyways, I do have two ghost stories that are associated with the University.

The first story deals with an apparition that appeared to two of my friends in residence. We lived in Lennox/Addington in a section called Arts House. My two friends lived in a corner room where the encounter took place. The first friend saw the ghost first. It was late at night and he couldn't sleep. It was dark but the window let in some light from nearby lamp posts. He glanced over at the window and saw a tall, long haired man sitting in the chair beneath the window. He was startled and looked over at the other bed, his roommate was sound asleep. Looking back at the window the figure was gone. He told his roommate about this the next day but he just scoffed at him saying it was just hypnogogic.

A few weeks later the first friend went home for the weekend. My other friend then had a similar experience. He awoke in the middle of the night and saw someone sitting in the chair looking quite sad. He thought it was a neighbour who was of similar build and hair length. He asked the figure what it wanted but it didn't reply. Thinking his neighbour was drunk he just shook his head and went back to sleep. The next day he questioned the neighbour why he was in his room. The neighbour was baffled by this question saying he didn't go in his room (which was locked) and that he had been up all night talking with other people from Arts House.

These were the only times that the figure appeared. I don't think they made it up since they were reluctant to repeat it to others. It's been awhile since I heard this story (which was right after the events) but I believe it's a fairly accurate retelling. If I see these friends again I'll ask them about it.

The second story is more of a friend-of-a-friend-type story. And it's not really that detailed.

A friend of a friend's mother is on the housekeeping staff and she says that she and other staff are reluctant to go into the basement of

Blackwood Hall because of an overpowering feeling of being watched. It is the only building where this occurs but it is one of the older buildings.

I hope you enjoyed these and I'll send you more if I hear of any.

A VERY STRANGE EXPERIENCE

I first saw this story on the Internet in a website devoted to ghostly affairs. I corresponded with its author, Kelly Kirkland, and she readily agreed that I could publish the article (dated February 16, 1996). Then she supplied me with additional material (dated March 13, 1996).

Here are both of Kelly Kirkland's accounts of "A Very Strange Experience." You explain what happened to her!

A Very Strange Experience

Kelly Kirkland

Hello!

This is a true story that happened to me. I'm not sure what it was but it was really weird!

One day I was going to see my dad by train to Toronto. My train was scheduled to leave by 3:27 pm and my boyfriend Jon was supposed to drive me to the station. He had gone to the store to pick something up and he was not home yet when I was supposed to be on my way to the station. I was looking out the front door to watch for him and I was very upset that I was going to miss my train (I did!) and I finally saw him coming up the street. I turned around to get my suitcase and when I turned back around I expected him to be in the driveway and he wasn't.

By then I was furious and I started to flip out and wonder where the hell he went to. Did he drive by the house and keep going? Did he forget something at the store he went to? Anyway, he finally showed up about fifteen minutes after I saw him and I confronted him as he walked in the door. I asked him why he hadn't pulled in the driveway and he told me that he hadn't even been on the street! I said that I had seen him fifteen minutes ago and he still insisted that he hadn't been anywhere near the house!

I still can't figure out what happened that day. I swear up and down that I saw his car coming up the street with him driving it! His car is hard to mistake because it has white spots on the roof where the paint peeled off. It was a very strange experience and I won't forget it any time soon.

Hello!

I'm sorry I haven't written sooner. I broke up with my boyfriend Jon and I no longer have the freedom of the Internet. I'm on my Uncle Otto's computer so you can e-mail me here if you like.

I received your letter in the mail a few weeks ago, thank you. You flattered me with your praise of my writing. …

My aunt has some ghost stories to tell you too. You can e-mail her directly at this address. Her name is Susan Andersen.

Anyway, my Grandma's address is King St. in Chatham. I won't give the exact address for obvious reasons. It is a one and a half story house with white siding. It is approximately 100 years old. There are three rooms on the main floor. As you walk in the front door you are in the front hall, to the left there is the dining room, to the right are the stairs to go up. If you walk straight from the front door you will end up in the living room. If you keep going straight you will find yourself in the kitchen. In the back of the small kitchen there are the back steps to go outside, just before you get to the outside door there are a few more steps to go to the basement. In the basement there is my uncle's barber shop. Behind the shop is the back room of the basement where the washer and dryer are.

I now bring you up to the second floor. At the top of the stairs there is a small hallway with the main bedroom on the left, a small bedroom on the right and further down another small bedroom on the right with a bathroom on the end.

In the first small bedroom on the right there is a dark stain under the carpet that no matter how hard you scrub it won't come out. I was told that it only gets brighter.

I hope this helps you out and feel free to e-mail me at this address.

THE WAYS OF THE HIERARCHY

One day I received a long-distance telephone call from Elsie Kelly, a woman unknown to me. She has a pleasant voice and a reasonable manner, so we had a pleasant chat. She explained that she was contacting me because she felt that I would be receptive to learning about some of the "transmissions" that she has been receiving.

"Why me?" I asked.

She replied, "In my public library I saw a copy of your book, the one called *UFOs over Canada*, and I thought you would be interested in what was said to me."

She explained that for some years she has been receiving messages from another intelligence and that she had arranged to have these printed in book form.

"When it is printed, send me a copy of the book," I replied. "I will be pleased to purchase it as well as reimburse you for the cost of the postage."

"Oh, it has already been printed. Shall I send it?"

"Please do!"

Now when I order books through the mail, it generally takes weeks or even months for purchases to arrive. So I was pleasantly surprised when only a couple of days later, in a packaged postmarked Peterborough, Ontario, came a copy of a neatly printed book of 306 pages. That evening I read it.

Let me describe its contents. Ms. Kelly's book has a pale blue cover. It is titled *Ways of the Hierarchy on Earth* and it bears the subtitle "A Guide to Spirituality." It was produced "In Preparation for the Battle of Armageddon." The subject of Armageddon was very much in the air and in the news just prior to Y2K. (As I am writing this, the subject has been eclipsed by 9/11.) So I checked the copyright page of

Ms. Kelly's book and found that it was copyright in the year 1998. The book is composed of three series of transmissions or, for want of a better word, dictations.

There is a four-fold organization of *Ways of the Hierarchy on Earth*. The first section (the shortest) describes the Society for the Betterment of Mankind, which is a global organization under spiritual direction that is preparing the human race and other forms of life on Earth for the changes that are to come.

This is a very serious section, so it was not leavened with humour. But I did find one detail that was amusing. A page is devoted to the locations of the Society's chapters, including the following centres: Egypt: Alexandria, Africa, New Zealand, Venezuela, New Mexico, Capernaum, Virgin Islands, and Canada: Toronto & Deseronto. This must be the first time that the town of Deseronto, located southwest of Napanee in the Bay of Quinte region of Ontario, has been designated in a spiritual text as a site special to mankind!

Then I remembered an historical parallel: There is a local tradition among the Indian bands of the region that it was near the present site of Deseronto that grew the original tree that had been uprooted by Dekanahwideh and Hiawatha to establish the Great Peace of the Iroquois Confederacy some four or five centuries ago. Perhaps the Native site and the Society are related.

The second section, the bulk of the book, consists of almost four hundred short meditations (if you wish) on subjects that range from "Acquiring Diligence" and "Abuse of Mothers" to "Youth to the Rescue" and "Yesterday." Between them are disquisitions on "Channeling" and "Christ Within," "Wantonness" and "Warriors of Our Lord." These are thoughtful little essays with a Christian flavour to the vocabulary.

The third section, a short one, offers the reader some parables, each with a message about thoughtfulness and love.

The fourth section is the one that will detain us here because it is so visionary. In this way it is unlike the first section, which is practical and devoted to the Society, or the second section, which recommends attitudes that are appropriate, or the third section, which offers moralistic messages. Instead, the fourth section is vivid and visionary. It consists of information previously uncommitted to print. Who or what constitutes the intelligence behind the transmission of this knowledge is unknown, but Ms. Kelly is its revelator.

The section consists of fifty-seven short entries. Some of these entries offer prefatory information, but about fifty of them are descriptions of unknown planets, their characteristic features, and the characteristics of their inhabitants. With Ms. Kelly's permission, I am reprinting a dozen or so of these entries, the ones devoted to descriptions of these planets. Perhaps I should put quotation marks around the word "planets," since only a few of these celestial bodies conform to those that are recognized by astronomers. In this regard I find that Ms. Kelly resembles the eighteenth-century Swedish scientist and seer Emanuel Swedenborg, who offered descriptions of the "spirit world," including views of Heaven and Hell, and descriptions of the souls that inhabit these domains.

Here are the accounts of these solar or galactic bodies, along with the Foreword that Ms. Kelly contributed to the work as a whole. It perhaps describes her situation and predicament — perhaps not hers alone — and it certainly conveys specific and general spiritual and extraterrestrial concerns.

Ways of the Hierarchy on Earth

Elsie Kelly

"Foreword: Worthy of a New Beginning"

There was a woman, who had three children, two girls and one boy. Her husband was not in good standing in the community and had adhered to the evils, wherein his contributions were nil. She, on her part, was exhausted by the constant demands of the children and her husband. Nevertheless, she continued on and did the best she could under trying circumstances.

One day, a great revelation came to her. Night after night, she would awaken to the sound of a flute. Dismayed with her hearing, she sought medical help, but without any luck. She happened to read of a similar case, about someone who had read the Teachings of the Far East. She then realized she was being summoned by a Master. With pen and tablet in hand, she began to write. Message after message she received, until the contents were in book form and published. Many benefited from her writings. She took no credit for the contents, but informed all, she was merely an instrument for their heavenly Father and Saviour. Many were envious and tried to bring her down in the face of others.

Before the turn of the century, great havoc came to Earth in the form of Nature's revenge. High winds, earthquakes, fires, etc., took many lives and soon all lay in unkempt reduction, all that was once a beautiful landscape. Thus, those who remained were only those of pious ways.

The book became their instrument of revelation, peace descended on Earth and once again a new beginning.

"Understanding of Entities in Galaxies"

Heavenly is the Light of Understanding, but a stalemate can be reached and all is then lost. Understanding in weakness of others is high for everyone concerned. Little or no understanding of not only themselves, but others in the galaxy.

Heretofore, many lived isolated and for billions of years were unable to anticipate any new arrivals within their boundaries. Even when a new being approached, suspicion was high on the agenda. Many more years went by, until establishment through marriage existed. This is also the case today.

Earth is surrounded by alien beings, wishing to make peace with Earth. Wishing to share their experiments to give added life to the planet, but yet suspicion arises. There are also Beings of supreme mind, who could give rest and comfort to those who are extremely ill from health problems. Their life span could be spread over many, many years ahead. This would be possible, if only the alien beings could be accepted and greeted in a brotherly manner.

It is true, the bodies of the space aliens are not of the physical bodies of Earth. Many operate on very slight stature, which is all that is necessary for their home planet. Within their being, their hearts abound with Love and Goodwill. Love of Mankind, regardless of outward appearance, is all which our Master of Masters requires.

Therefore, please Earth, accept our goodwill. If so, we can progress at such a high rate of speed, that all wars would cease. Rest would envelope like a blanket of loving understanding.

Sacred and Non-sacred Planets

There are planets within our galaxy which house all types of consciousness from the very lowest to the highest. Of those, the lowest are called non-sacred planets, of which Earth is one. Pluto is also a non-sacred planet. It lies between that of the righteous and that of evil content. It marks the way of the soul and shows the way of the future attainment, if desired.

There is always one incarnation, which is a ruling one. It decides, whether the soul remains in a low or high standing. Great are the traverses and high are the values, if throughout this life the soul plods steadily onward, on to a higher goal. Therefore, do not consider boundaries toward soul attainment. Consider them as obstacles, placed on one's path. This will allow determination to overcome. Then future attainments are in sight. Hinder not by self-pity. If not overcome, it could prove as a block of misery and no further advancement can be made.

Alexandreaus

The planet of the greatest interest to Earth is the planet Alexandreaus. It is located in the part of the galaxy, which is commonly known as the tail of the Bull, Taurus. The axis of the planet rotates at an amazing speed. The climate fluctuations hardly allow the fields to ripen before another onslaught of freezing rain envelopes all. Major changes of climate prevents anyone or anything to live on the surface. All cities are located in the centre of the planet.

Interior light is reflected from the core of the fire. Great is the inner to science, but poor is the quality of the physical bodies. Many lives lived in extreme poverty. They are deprived of the necessities of life. The leader of the populace is the Lord of Matter, who possesses unbelievable fortitude and compassion. Through His study of compassionate understanding, great strides have been made in eliminating many of the diseases. Therefore, on this planet, the care for humanity continues to flourish.

Earth is outstanding and known as a planet of both good and evil. It is on Earth that the population lives on the surface. However, the time has come, when the evil shall stand out. The retaliation by the good shall succeed.

Arkavantitus

There is a planet known as Arkavantitus. It is located in the far end of our galaxy. It has a populace of twelve million. It is small in size, but has a beauty, unseen by many. The trees and foliage are of a soft green. The blue shades of the sky and seas have never been seen by anyone on Earth or elsewhere. It is here, the children of Israel once dwelt as angels. They flitted here and there, like beautiful birds. They traversed from one port of the planet to another. Their voices lifted in song. Radiant were their bodies, clothed in garments of gold. One by one they drifted to Earth. Their souls were encased in physical bodies. Immediately after physical death, they went to yet another newly born baby. They are still encased. Each body on Earth is a holder of such a prisoner.

Not until one's thoughts are to the needs of others can these babes-in-arms be freed from Earth. They can then return once again to their heaven. Try as one might, it is difficult to understand the truth of the statement. You are not alone. You hold sweetness and love as captives in your heart.

Balestravia

Balestravia is a tiny speck in the heavens, on the other side of the galaxy. It teems with life and everything, which exists on Earth, also exists on that planet. It is the duplication of every human, animal, bird, etc. It is the counterpart, wherein souls of Earth visit during their sleeping periods. They awaken in Balestravia and do their duties. It is a continuation of their spirit. Never does the spirit rest. Their forms are identical. However, they take on the attitudes of the secret fantasies formed during their awakened state on Earth.

Great are their actions in an evil mode. Try as they might, they cannot escape, until sleep claims them and they awaken again on Earth. They then call them dreams or nightmares.

In reality, they are merely the continuation of the spirit's journey through space. Those of high virtues, go to other planets. Whatever plateau of consciousness, there is a planet of dual nature. Be careful of what one wishes for, it will come true during the sleeping state.

Cararus

There is a planet known as Cararus. Its population is of a startling appearance. They are of little stature, but their strength is of an amazing description. Their legs are short, but have bulging biceps. They have an immensely huge upper body, but the lower body is very short. It has the appearance of almost non-existence. Their heads are huge, are almost the same size as their torsos. Their complexions are blue. Their eyes and ears are depleted. They mobilize only by sound, which comes through the centre of their forehead. The sound enters through two slits, which also serve as nostrils. They do not have what is known as a mouth, but only a slit. This takes in the particles of sand, which contain their necessary vitamins.

They are a particular breed, known for their loving ways. The outer appearance to a stranger approaching is stupendous, but looking deeper, there is everything in the way of a pious nature. Therefore, do not judge by outer eye, but the inner eye of our beloved Lord and Master Jesus.

Caratusias

There is a planet known as Caratusias. It is the planet, which is known for its intensity of speed. Everything turns at a high rate and Earth does not compare in any way.

From dawn to dusk, the populace is forced to gear every moment to the maximum. Its success is known throughout the universe. Great is the disaster, if only one does not comply.

Factories manufacture the needs not only for themselves, but for other planets as well. The population is staggering, compared to earth. They migrate in droves once a year and copulate, never knowing the father of the child. Not even the father is aware of his offspring. The copulation is devoid of an emotional value. It is a duty. It is considered part of their endeavour to fill the void, left by early death, due to their life style. They are also devoid of a high mental state and act as robots.

Therefore, value your high standing on planet Earth. The other populace know nothing of any other planet, but serve in their own way. Their souls will pass on to a high level, when transition is made at their physical death.

Flemosania

Flemosania is a small planet, located close to the universal hangar, known as Venatia. It is considered the highest of dwellings.

The population consists of those who have contributed the highest of value throughout their incarnations. It is the last planet to reside on, before leaving our Gemini Solar System.

Many are those who were implicated in wars or who performed fetes, in which our Lord was held in high favour. Many served as a servant and suffered great abuse in His name. Today, they are the kings, owning more than gold. They possess the love of God, which nestles within their hearts. Each heart is bursting with happiness.

Keep always the love of God deep within one's heart, for it is like a flame, ready to be fanned.

Graphicus

This planet is of dire appearance. All is in varying shades of gray. Even the inhabitants share this same fate. Sober are their surroundings, the same, as was their state on Earth.

During their prior life, they never gave consideration to others. Their main thought was of themselves, and their envy of others was like a deadly drink throughout each day. If happiness was revealed by another, a smoldering envious thought remained. If awakened during the night, this same thought controlled their nature.

Hence the removal to one of the non-sacred planets in the galaxy. It is here they will remain for eons of time after their physical death on Earth.

Olisapede

Olisapede is located near the entrance of the Milky Way and close to the universe of Terrapelen. It is of an unusual size and shape, compared to other planets. It is square in appearance and has a peculiar aura. The aura is not unlike a vapour and has many varied colours. These colours have never been experienced by the human eye on Earth.

The individuals, who abide on this planet, have feet of enormous size. A high rate of gravity maintains their upright position. They speak in muted voices, and only when necessary. Other than that, they remain at a discreet distance apart.

Once a year, they meet to cohabit, therefore guaranteeing an increase in the populace. This is thought of as a necessary chore, rather than a celebration.

Their main purpose is the climbing of the high mountains to find food for existence. Their food consists of a certain mineral, found only on the plateaus. Many fall into deep gorges, but enough are saved to carry on with their existence.

Low are they on the totem pole. However, after serving only one incarnation, they are then placed on another planet, only a little above in value. This is the gradual stance toward awareness of others.

We all began our existence on this planet and so it will be for others.

Parusicedes

Parusicedes is not unlike Mars. It is a non-sacred planet, devoid of all who have attained even a small amount of Christ Consciousness.

The inhabitants are only interested in wood carving. Their substance is gained by the dust accumulated. It is sewn into sacks and distributed to the populace.

These are not the humanoids. They are worm-like in appearance and do not stand upright. They multiply at an alarming speed. All are devoid of eyes and use only the scent of the wood to discern the difference of their menu.

Many incarnations are needed before a slight improvement is made. Only those who stand upright are considered worthy to reincarnate on another planet.

Platemus

Platemus is known for its wide and extensive knowledge of the workings of the universe.

The inhabitants are pink in colour. They spend many hours over maps and calculations. They can and do guide space travellers on their way to all parts of the universe. Great honour is taken in knowing not a planet exists, that is not recorded. Happy are those who arrive and are given directions to their next stopping point.

Today, much is in flux. Many planets are now without inhabitants. The surface on many planets is being ejected, due to the cracking of the top soil. The souls of these planets are now emerging. Very few respond to the name of our Lord and therefore they must be banished.

Wynonalis

Wynonalis is known for its beauty. All on Wynonalis are outstanding in their understanding of the wildlife, which abounds. Animals and birds share an abundance of colour. From a distance, this star is breathtaking in all its glory.

Few understand the quaintness, in which all live and respect each other. They knowingly allow respect for all their boundaries. Happiness is thought of as an every day way of life. If only Earth could know, what awaits all, who become sacred planets, they would stand in awe. Souls now living with these exceptional animals and birds, all share such beauty. Their population consists strictly of souls, who are placed there, because of their outstanding virtue. They will at one point leave and be placed on another star, to carry on their work for our heavenly Father.

Zarotophus

Zarotophus lies between Earth and Saturn and cannot be seen by the human eye. It is of etheric matter and receives the souls of those of lesser mentality. They are held as children in a play-like setting. Never aggressive, but always loving in spirit, they play and rest throughout their days. They will need this tranquility before entering the battlefield of Earth and like planets.

Their minds have been dulled due to inheriting a brain disease, passed on by one of their parents. They cannot rationalize right from wrong, but appear with a soul of beauty, which can be seen by all. They are innocent, as they were on the day, when they were in our Father's house.

Blessed are they in the eyes of the Lord.

FERGUS IN GOOD SPIRITS

When I published *Mysterious Canada*, way back in 1988, I explained that the Ontario town of Niagara-on-the-Lake was the most haunted community in Canada. I went on to explain that there are no agencies that compile statistics on reports of hauntings; StatsCan has never heard of ghosts! I also added that the picturesque town and home of the Shaw Festival is the country's most haunted community on a per capita basis. Obviously a metropolis like Toronto has more ghosts than Niagara-on-the-Lake, but taking into account the ratio of ghosts to humans, the small town wins hands down.

A decade later, when I published *Mysteries of Ontario*, I knew otherwise. Niagara-on-the-Lake is a haunted community, to be sure, but on a per capita basis the spectral laurels go to the even smaller Ontario town of Fergus. So, in my opinion today, Fergus is the most haunted community in the country.

Making this claim on radio or television, I am often asked why this is so, or why I believe this is so. My response goes like this: Fergus has so many ghosts, its Chamber of Commerce has issued a guide to them — a first for any community. The dead haunt the living by a ratio of 1:1,000, a very high ratio to be sure. Perhaps behind this is the fact that this area of south-central Ontario, with its rich farmland, was settled by the Highland Scots who, in addition to being hard-working, work hard at preserving their Old Country traditions, and among these are the traditions of haunted houses.

No single account can bring across the richness of Fergus's heritage of spirits. So to illustrate it, I will reprint here an article written by Jack Kohane, photographer, journalist, and friend. When I purchased a photo of Jack's for use in my book *Haunted Toronto*, I had no idea that the sale would lead to commissions to photograph other places for

Mysteries of Ontario, and Jack had no idea he would begin to write about ghosts and spirits he encountered on his travels throughout southern Ontario writing about spas, inns, hotels, motels, and bed-and-breakfast establishments. The article was written in 1999.

Ghost Hunter Keeps Fergus in Good Spirits

Jack Kohane

Pat Mestern believes in ghosts. Living in Fergus, Ontario (population 8,500), reputedly the town with more haunted houses per capita than anywhere else in Canada, she couldn't be closer to the paranormal action. As the resident ghost hunter, Mestern's the one to call when things go bump — and crash and shriek and thud — in the night.

In all other respects Fergus, located northwest of Toronto, is postcard perfect. Originally founded in the early 1800s, it never relinquished its position as the county's agricultural and industrial hub. Fergus treasures its past, preserving its historical architecture passionately. More than 100 magnificent century-plus stately homes and buildings nuzzle tranquilly against serene, tree-shaded streets.

But Mestern attests to more ethereal elements lurking behind those stone facades. She relishes telling her most vivid encounters with the spirit world.

The most famous case involves the Wellington County Museum. This impressive edifice is perched atop a hill overlooking the roaring Grand River. For a century after its construction in 1877 it was known as the House of Industry & Refuge, the poorhouse. Rumours abounded for decades of gruesome medical experiments conducted on inmates, some who went mad, and others who escaped into a winter night only to die slowly of hypothermia.

In 1979, Mestern was among a group of 20 people, together with a video crew, permitted to spend the night at the museum. The creaky old building was legendary for its eerie nocturnal clamors. Cameras whirred throughout the building.

"As the evening wore on, nothing happened and we grew bored," recalls Mestern. "Suddenly, at the stairs leading to the rear attic (where no one was stationed), came the thud of footsteps. A cameraman sputtered a string of expletives. On his TV monitor, there was the pale image of a shadowy figure. Several of us raced into the room, and stopped dead. We saw nothing, but felt gripped by a bone-chilling cold as if something had passed right through us. As heat gradually returned, we stood trembling, speechless, unable to describe what had just touched us."

Later, a renowned psychic visiting the museum described to Mestern some of the unhappy spirits "trapped" there, identifying at least three ghostly entities haunting the structure. In addition to footsteps of unknown origin plodding the stairwells repeatedly on certain nights, there is the dowager "Matron" walking the main floor; an old lady in a spectral rocking chair in the east gallery; and a sobbing woman on the second floor.

In her home on St. David Street, Mestern experienced another, more personal incident. One summer afternoon as she slept on her living room sofa, a rush of frigid air awoke her. Instantly transfixed, she saw a wizened old woman dressed in a long gown with frilly lace collar gliding towards her. "She had an unnerving stare," says Mestern. "I was fully awake. Before I could speak, she vanished." Later, by coincidence, a man Mestern never met sent her a photograph taken in 1900 of his long-dead relative who once resided in Fergus. The house in the picture's background was indeed the present Mestern residence, and the woman glaring at the camera was also unmistakable — those piercing eyes were the same that glowered at Mestern on that dreadful day. The portrait now hangs over the hallway steps, the woman disconcertingly eyeing all who enter.

One of the most extraordinary cases to come to Mestern's attention surrounds a 170-year-old dwelling on Fergus's eastern perimeter. Gloria Kavanagh, who lived in the big stone house during the 1980s, frantically contacted Mestern when the "problems" started. "It began soon after when we moved in," Gloria shudders at the memories. "First, fits of coughing and sneezing erupted from the attic, but no one was up there. For many nights, boots were heard trudging overhead. One evening, my daughter saw an old man standing in her doorway. He wore an army hat, a strange uniform, and his rifle pointed menacingly into the room." By the description of the clothes, Mestern determined it was similar to that worn by British soldiers during the Boer War in South Africa a century ago. A deceased resident of the house, it was discovered, had in fact fought in that conflict.

Gloria continues: "Often when we arrived home at night, we could hear the scurrying of feet, like a youngster running away. Occasionally a chair in the kitchen would sway back and forth as if someone was rocking in it. Some nights we were startled awake by what sounded like a party downstairs. My husband shouted from bed for the noise to stop — it did. The next day we saw no signs of revelry."

The Kavanaghs had enough and moved to another house several miles away, but even there peace remains elusive. "Periodically, there's rapping on our bedroom door," Gloria's voice wavers. "Books fall off the shelf and there's no one nearby. I've come home to an empty house to find baking soda strewn all over the kitchen floor, and on one occasion a flower pot rack literally flew by itself across the hallway and crashed against a wall." On the evidence, Mestern speculates the Kavanaghs are plagued by the spirit of a child playing pranks to gain attention for some unknown reason.

Another fabled Fergus haunt is Kinnettles, the first house (circa 1837) erected on the west side of Fergus. Named after the original builder's home in Scotland, today it has a more ominous title: "The Ghost House." The accounts began in 1879, when the remains of an unknown woman, clad only in a nightgown, were discovered behind the house. The body was brought into the living room and the coroner summoned. But before he arrived, the corpse vanished. To this day, no one knows for sure why the body was taken. The mystery, which created a major sensation in Victorian-era Ontario, remains unsolved today.

Kinnettles was abandoned for many years following that episode. There were grisly tales of blood flowing like streams across the floors, and black slime oozing from its walls. The current owners insist they've seen nothing odd. Mestern asserts that such manifestations are usually associated with a particular item. "With that object gone or removed from the house, the source of the haunting also departs," she says.

In Mestern's view Fergus isn't extraordinary. "My theory is that a haunting can occur anywhere," she says. "Events of the past, present and future can converge in any locale, and everyone leaves a wisp of something behind when they die. But I don't believe in poltergeists or malevolent ghosts."

What's happening in Fergus is attributable to the story-telling tradition among the Scots, says John Robert Colombo, paranormal aficionado and author of *Mysterious Canada*, *Haunted Toronto*, and the upcoming *Mysteries of Ontario*. "The town has a rich Scottish past, and with a relatively stable and homogenous population, legends accumulate. Further, haunted houses are also a powerful tourist attraction."

"Most of my neighbors think I'm crazy," smiles Mestern. "But I don't care. I grew up here and understand this town intimately. I know there are ghosts here — lots of them."

The Fergus Chamber of Commerce provides a booklet (photocopy only) titled "The Fergus Self-Guided Ghost Tour," which describes other haunted sites clustered along the town's heritage-filled main street. For more information call 519-843-5140, or write the Chamber: 100 Queen Street East, P.O. Box 3, Fergus, Ontario N1M 2W7.

IT WAS AN AMAZING EXPERIENCE

Late one night, perusing the website "X Archives" on the Internet, on November 5, 1995, I found this unusual story. I have given it the following title: "It Was an Amazing Experience."

I know nothing about the author, who signed himself "Ekin," but I secured permission from the moderator of the newsgroup to run his story in this slightly edited form.

For readers with Internet access who are interested in reading similar personal accounts of hauntings, the address to use is as follows: *http://www.crown.net/X/Stories/GSGhost.html*

It Was an Amazing Experience

"Ekin"

I am new to this and I liked the info on paranormal activity, so I thought I would share my own experience.

About a year ago, while working at a gas station known as The Beehive here in Sarnia, Ontario, CA, I came across various stories on the history of the building. Most notably were the painted-over sign that read "Methodist Church, 1886" and the fact that the place used to be a hotel (one of our customers was born there). However, the site has been a gas station/variety store for many years now.

One story that stood out was that one of the original owners of The Beehive practically lived in the back room of the building with his cot, stove, etc., till one day he had a heart attack and passed away. Since that time, there have been a couple of owners, but I did not come into employment till after the newest owner took over. Many renovations have been made, including the relocation of one of the doorways. (You can still see where the door was.)

One evening, while working with another co-worker, standing side-by-side, cleaning shelves, we witnessed something that made me ever so excited. From the spot of the old doorway, we both happened to witness an image of someone walking through the doorway and behind the counter before vanishing. When it was gone, we both looked at each other, pale as (excuse the pun) ghosts. I became excited and intrigued and ran over there. My co-worker just stood there in shock. She quickly denied the whole thing, but I truly do believe I saw a ghost, possibly of the old owner. I have yet to see a photo of that person to compare it to what I saw.

It was an amazing experience, no matter how short. I hope it occurs again.

THE P.E.I. HAUNTINGS

Here is an informal account of four hauntings that occurred on the campus of the University of Prince Edward Island at Charlottetown.

It is the first Canadian ghost story that I collected from the Internet. That must be half a dozen years ago now. E-mail lends itself to spontaneity of expression and informality of manner.

I found it on the newsgroup *Alt.ghost-stories*. The accounts were posted by someone who was a student at the time, David K. MacKinnon of Charlottetown, P.E.I.

The P.E.I. Hauntings

David K. MacKinnon

This has been a while in coming, but here it is.

1.

During my time at the University of Prince Edward Island, Charlottetown, I have heard of a number of campus hauntings. As background, our campus used to be two campuses, St. Dunstan's University and Prince of Wales College. The two amalgamated in the late 1960's (1968, I believe) to form the only university in this province.

The first dates back to when the building currently in use by the Home Economics department was used as a male residence. On this particular night, two students were in the town having a high old time. A snowstorm began to blow up and they started back. One was slower than the other, so he asked his friend to go on ahead and make sure the door was open because he knew he would not make it back before cur-few when the front door would be locked. The friend went on ahead and made it just before the door was locked, but he was banished to his room for being so late.

Later, the second roommate arrived to find the door locked and no way to get in. He pounded on the door, but the priests would not let him in, intending to teach him a lesson. An hour or so later, the first roommate, worried for his friend, heard a knock at the dorm room door. He went up to answer it. All that greeted him was a cold draft of air. He looked down to see a trail of water leading to the staircase from his doorway. Puzzled, he returned to bed.

The next morning, the second roommate was found frozen to death outside the front door.

Ever since that night, staff or students who are working late in the building during a particularly blustery winter's night may find a cold breeze blow past them, and look down to see the same trail of water leading from a particular room to the staircase.

Such is the tale of Dalton Hall.

2.

The next story is a more uplifting. It concerns the Cass Chemistry building. Father Cass was a benevolent soul and a caring teacher who lived during the early part of the century. When he died, the building was named in his honour, as he had spent most of his life teaching chemistry to the college's varied population. It is said that Father Cass still roams the halls, looking after his students, even those who were born long after his death.

One night, two chemistry students were working late on a project. Despite the rule that no one is allowed to work alone in the building in case something happens, one student decided to make a quick run down to the local Burger King for something almost but not quite entirely unlike food to tide them over through the wee early hours. The second student was left on the top floor to look after the experiment.

Not long after the first student left, the second heard a noise from downstairs. Thinking it might be his/her partner, he went downstairs to see who was there. (Before I go any further, you must understand that there is one staircase inside the building, thus one way from the main level to the top. The fire escape is accessible from the second floor and up, but has never been used due to its advanced state of disrepair. There would be no way for a person to get through the building without being seen or heard. Also consider that sound travels *very* well in this empty building at night.)

To return to the story, he went downstairs to see who it was. Not finding anyone, or hearing anyone in the building, he went back upstairs. There he found the Bunsen burner that had been left running was shut off, the gas shut down both at the nozzle and the wall, and the tube neatly rolled up. It was then that this student remembered the stories of Father Cass putting things away that were left unattended.

3.

There is only one other historic haunting I can think of, but we refuted it with a bit of investigation. Apparently in the Main Building, before it was renovated, a certain room would be seen from the outside to have a light on. Not so strange you say, but if you look closely you can see a figure hanging from the ceiling.

Apparently, one of the professors had hanged himself in that room. Ever since then, the room could be seen from the outside to be lit. It revealed a dim figure swinging slowly on the end of a rope from the ceiling. If you tried to find the room, you would find the only door into it covered with boxes. Remove the boxes and unlock the door and you would find an empty light socket.

As I said, we disproved this. There was another way into the room.

4.

The last story I will relate is a bit hard for me to believe, even though I was there. I am a skeptic by nature. I believe there probably is more to this world than meets the eye. Psychic powers may be possible, though I see precognition as being incredibly perceptive and being able to deduce the future based on a paranormal knowledge of what is happening in the world (beyond normal human perception, that is).

It has been said by the women of Bernadine Hall, the campus's women's residence, that the lounge on the fourth floor is a focus for spirits. Of this I'm skeptical, but I have an open mind, so I'll reserve my disbelief until I see proof either way.

On one particular night, we decided to try a seance using the Ouija board. Now, I have been described as being an excellent receiver, and this was one of the reasons why they wanted me involved. Once I was asked to try to describe a house as a friend of mine "walked" through it in his mind. I was able to describe the house in detail, down to the colour and style of furniture and the geodesic dome in the back yard. I've not been able to explain it, but I hadn't yet seen the place. I'll reserve my judgement of what I saw until then.

Back to the story. Several of us took part in this, taking turns (male with female) on the board to see if we could find anything. Soon, we started feeling cold, and one of the more sensitive of the group began to take on a different personality. Now, we were all trying to be open to spirits. I was trying my hand at automatic writing as this was happening. The person affected was at the Ouija board. He began to talk as if he were a scared young girl. At the same time, I and another friend got this incredibly clear vision of a room in this building, but we could feel it was on the other side of the building on the third floor. My vision was of looking out over a bed from a black room to an open doorway. Standing in the doorway was a young woman wearing a skirt to just below the knee and shoulder length hair. The light from the hallway was shining in behind her. I could feel fear of … the girl? Something anyway … and a feeling that I had to get past her into the light.

At the same time, one of the women had a vision of looking onto a dark room on the opposite side of the building at a young woman cowering behind a bed. The feeling she received was of concern for the girl, who looked to be terrified, but of what she didn't know.

These stories were heard by an independent witness, so we would not trade information. I'm at a loss to explain them. Was it a vision of a person cowering in fear, or did we simply have a psychically linked dream? Or did the independent witness collaborate with my friend to match her story to mine? I guess I'll never know.

127

By the way, the person who became "possessed" was faking it. Or at least he appeared to be faking.

If you know of any other UPEI stories, I'd be happy to hear them, or any stories relating to Eastern Canada.

THE HAUNTING EXPERIENCE

I am indebted to Robert Buckman for the following account, which I have titled "The Haunting Experience." Dr. Buckman is an oncologist, humanist, broadcaster, and author.

In the chapter titled "The Neurology of Belief" in his book *Can We Be Good without God? Biology, Behaviour and the Need to Believe* (Buffalo: Prometheus Press, 2002), Dr. Buckman refers to the ground-breaking work of the neurosurgeon Wilder Penfield of Montreal in stimulating the temporal lobes of patients with electric probes during brain surgery. He found that the right temporal lobe produced a variety of experiences, perceptions, and feelings. As Dr. Buckman noted, "The conclusion was inescapable that the right temporal lobe was a crucial component in our process of perception — in all modalities — and in the process by which we are conscious of ourselves and of things around us."

Dr. Buckman then turned his attention to the intriguing and important research undertaken by Dr. Michael Persinger, professor of neuroscience, Laurentian University, Sudbury, Ontario.

> Persinger stimulated the right temporal lobe not by using an electric current in the Penfield manner but by creating complex electromagnetic fields that were basically electromagnetic imitations or models of temporal lobe epilepsy. When these imitation temporal lobe seizures were "played back" into the temporal lobes of volunteers by using magnetic solenoids built into a helmet, the person's temporal lobe was essentially immersed in an electromagnetic atmosphere very similar to that of temporal lobe epilepsy, the intensity of which could be adjusted by Persinger at will.

129

Dr. Persinger found that there is a variety of responses and that some people are more sensitive to temporal lobe stimulation than others. Responses could range from epileptic-style seizures to episodes described as "absences" to openness to "imaginary worlds." Dr. Buckman noted, "The more sensitive your temporal lobe is, the more likely it is that you will have regular (and deep) religious experiences." Dr. Persinger went on to develop a Personal Philosophy Inventory to correlate belief and behaviour with temporal lobe lability.

Dr. Buckman summarized Dr. Persinger's findings with respect to thought, feeling, sensation, and behaviour by listing fourteen characteristics of "what the right temporal lobe does." The characteristics are Dr. Buckman's; the additional explanatory phrases are my versions of his.

1. Auditory experiences: hearing sounds or voices; suffering auditory hallucinations.
2. Visual experiences: seeing lights, patterns, and colours, sometimes images associated with one's past.
3. Vestibular experiences: sensing movement, changes in orientation or position.
4. Taste and smell experiences: noting the presence of odours or scents either familiar or unfamiliar.
5. Memory changes: experiencing incongruous *déjà-vu* or *jamais vu*.
6. Extracorporeal experiences: perceiving oneself to be outside one's own body.
7. Morning highs: waking up in the morning extremely elated.
8. Drama, poetry, and other creative acts: involving oneself in artistic expression, entering "another world."
9. Sense of presence: feeling that one is in the presence of another intelligence, possibly that of a god or a ghost.
10. Other religious and spiritual experiences: entering into a deep, spiritual experience that includes a sense of peacefulness and an understanding of the cosmos.
11. Signs of special significance: reading into events and experiences a special meaning or message for oneself alone.

12. Pseudocyesis (false pregnancy): experiencing the cessation of menstrual periods with signs of pregnancy when not pregnant.
13. Near-death experiences: seeing the "white light" or experiencing other sensations traditionally associated with the approach of death.
14. "I would kill in God's name": assenting to any act, including murder, based on the certainty that God exists and has commanded one to perform it.

Dr. Persinger's findings are remarkable for what they reveal about "the neurology of belief" as well as what might be termed "the neurology of behaviour." His findings will presumably be reproduced in other laboratories.

In the meantime, Dr. Buckman offers the case history of "a journalist and broadcaster" and his ghostly experience (presumably characteristics numbers 2 and 3 from the listing of temporal lobe experiences above). He writes, "Since I had an opportunity to discuss the experiences in detail with the person who underwent them, I shall take the liberty of setting the case out in some detail."

The Haunting Experience

Robert Buckman

The subject is a journalist and broadcaster and was in his early forties when he moved into a house in Alberta that would be called — in the general use of the word — "haunted." He had had no personal previous experiences of ghosts or hauntings, and was not particularly inclined to give credibility to stories of the supernatural.

In the first years in the haunted house, he noticed several things which he regarded as unusual and "creepy." There were noises and bangs in the nights (perhaps this is not very unusual in older houses) and electric light bulbs would suddenly go dim or burn very brightly, and he thought that some would glow even when they were turned off. On at least one occasion, a light bulb shattered without warning. None of these events are in themselves unique.

However, the most signal experience was when, together with a friend of his, he investigated a crawl space in the basement. Both men thought they saw an apparition — although, significantly, they each described it differently. However, both of them experienced at the same moment a feeling of great dread and, basically, terror and panic. Neither of them had ever experienced anything like it before, and neither of them had ever felt they had seen a ghost or had had an experience of anything that they would have described as supernatural.

Shortly afterward, the subject sold that house — for reasons that included the experiences — and moved many thousands of miles away.

Four years after this single experience of "haunting," while working as a journalist, he came into contact with Michael Persinger who volunteered to try the "temporal lobe" helmet with the solenoids in it as described above.

Extraordinarily, in his case, when the solenoids were activated and the electromagnetic fields were created in the helmet, he experienced an almost exact "replay" or recreation of the haunting experience. In particular, the same emotions experienced at the haunting were aroused when the electromagnetic field was switched on in the helmet. The subject felt exactly the same sense intensity of dread, terror, and panic. At that moment he also felt quite clearly that there was a presence in the laboratory room with him. The emotions and that feeling both disappeared when the electromagnetic field was turned off.

He is quite certain that he had only had two experiences like this — the first in the basement of his house in Alberta, the second while undergoing electromagnetic stimulation of the temporal lobe in Persinger's laboratory four years later.

IT LEAVES ONE WONDERING

Chance, happenstance, coincidence, stroke of luck, godsend, miracle, good fortune, serendipity ... the English language offers many words for what might or might not be instances of design in human affairs.

Here is a vivid account of luck or providence in action. The Swiss psychologist Carl Jung would have used his own word to describe what Karin and Andrew discovered, and that word is simultaneity. Happenings that are not causally connected but are meaningfully interconnected are instances of simultaneities. Here is one example of simultaneity originally released on the Internet.

It Leaves One Wondering

Karin Dearness

The following is a recounting of an actual chain of events that took place in my home three years ago. Make of it what you will....

It all began when my friend, Andrew, offered to help my step-father reinsulate the attic of our hundred-year-old home. While they were removing the old insulation they found, underneath one of the bats, a stack of about twelve letters tied with ribbon. The letters were love letters from 1928 from a girl named Mary to a man named Adam Zimmerman who used to live at our house. The letters were written in rather olde-style English and done with a calligraphy pen. Because of this they were not easy to read.

Andrew and I stayed up all night transcribing the letters into the computer by having one person read and the other type. This took us most of Sunday night (till 4:00 a.m.!). We hadn't read the letters the day we found them since we were up to our ears in insulation and decided to save them for that evening.

We placed the letters in chronological order and began reading them as they were being transcribed. They were quite interesting. They detailed the relationship that Mary and Adam had in the summer of 1928 and how they would take the train to see each other. We gathered from the letters that Adam was somewhat older than Mary and that their relationship was not condoned by their parents. It was even hinted at that they may be cousins or distant relatives. At any rate, the letters were most engrossing.

We figured out that it was quite possible that Adam could still be alive and would be somewhere between eighty and ninety years old. The letters suggested that he wrote a lot of poetry and was planning to go to law school. Andrew and I decided that we would look up local records for Adam the following day (Monday) and see if we could return the letters to him.

Well, Monday came and went (we were both undergraduate students at the time and had a day's worth of lectures to go to). As usual, I picked up the paper on the way home, as Andrew and I were in the habit of doing the crossword puzzle. After doing the puzzle, we were sitting in the living room with two other house-mates joking about Mr. Zimmerman, wondering if he ever married Mary, became a lawyer, etc. ...

I thought it would be funny to pretend that I saw his name in the obituaries to spook my house-mates. I grabbed the obits and joking said "Suddenly yesterday ..." As they were chuckling, I noticed that the obits ended in the "T's," so I flipped over the page and there it was. Adam Zimmerman had died the previous day! I just screamed and instantly my friends knew I wasn't joking. From the description in the paper it seems quite clear that this was the same person. He did become a lawyer but didn't end up marrying Mary.

Could the two events be related? Perhaps so, perhaps not, but whichever, it leaves one wondering.

A HAUNTED HOUSE IN ROCKWOOD

Here are three e-mails. I received them in the year 2000, on January 7, January 19, and September 26. I am reproducing them here as they were received, though I have edited them somewhat for ease of reading.

They come from a correspondent named Angie Laurus. The answer to Angie's question about a haunted house in Rockwood is as follows: No, unfortunately I have no information on any "haunts" that are to be found in that community.

Rockwood is a charming place located not far from Guelph, Ontario. It has many houses of historical interest. One of those houses is the Rockwood Academy (which, by the looks of it, ought to be haunted!).

I wonder where *this* house is located.

A Haunted House in Rockwood

Angie Laurus

Morning!

Hope you can steer me in the right direction.

I have just recently ordered your book, *Ghost Stories of Ontario*, and anxiously wait for its arrival.

Did you by chance come across any stories about a haunted house in Rockwood, Ontario? The home was built in 1853 as a Quaker meeting place. It has since been used as a monastery, a bed and breakfast, and a private residence.

The locals insist the house is haunted. As some stories go, the monks used to store their dead in the cellar during winter months until the ground thawed. Some say that monks are buried in the cellar too.

There are also stories that there was a murder/suicide in the home. There are stories about a deranged boy who was in the care of the monks who died violently.

The list is endless.

My friend Danny has just moved into this home. Danny is not a believer of ghosts, but I feel he will be converted soon. Danny has recounted incidents for which there is no explanation except a supernatural one. Objects are knocked over or moved. Sudden changes in room temperature. A strong breeze through the room when all windows and doors are closed. The TV or radio volume is lowered. Footsteps heard overhead when no one else except Danny is home.

Danny was doing extensive renovations to the house. Contractors came on a Sunday to install siding. It was a beautiful calm sunny day. Danny heard a horrible scream and ran outdoors to find a contractor hanging from the side of the pool. After Danny rescued him, the worker told Danny that this sudden gust of wind came up and blew him off the scaffolding. The worker did not have a scratch or bruise on him. Neighbours say that the ghosts of the dead monks hold Sunday sacred and sabotage any work performed.

Danny would like to do some research on his home and hasn't a clue where to start. Any suggestions?

I would appreciate any help you may offer.

Thank you for your time.

Angie Laurus

Hi,

Yes, I did write to you some time back about a house my friend was renting.

The house is located in Rockwood. My friend has since moved out. As the story goes, it is haunted. The locals have some great stories to tell about it. Here's what I know about the house:

It was originally built by the Quakers and used as a meeting place.

It was a monastery at one time and rumours have it that monks were buried in the cellar.

The monks were guardians for a severely mentally challenged boy. The boy attacked his parents with a knife when they came to visit him. The parents locked themselves in a closet but their son continued to hack at the door. The door was still at the house when my friend lived there and you can see the gouges. I understand the boy died there.

There is also a story about a suicide. I believe it occurred when the house was a bed and breakfast.

My friend Danny told me lots of unexplained encounters with one or more ghosts.

The ghost or ghosts were friendly but mischievous. Made a lot of noise, turned lights off and on, TV and radio on and off, knocked items off shelves, and littered the floors with their contents. The list is endless.

Danny was never a believer in ghosts but is one now.

If you like, I can ask Danny to recount as many incidents as he can and pass them on to you.

Another friend still lives in Rockwood and I can ask him to find out as much as he can about the house.

Before I sign off, just want to mention that I enjoyed your book *Ghost Stories of Ontario* very much.

Take care,
Angie.

I checked my books and my files but could find no record of a haunted house in Rockwood, northeast of Guelph, Ontario, although in there are haunted sites in Rockton and Roebuck, and I have always felt that the Rockwood Academy, which dates back to the 1850s, was creepy enough to be haunted!

Sorry, Angie, no sites for you to check out!

People who experience anomalous phenomena in their residence should keep a log of everything that happens in and around the house — not just creepy things, but also renovations, visitors, changes in the weather, etc. That way you might find a cause or a pattern for the odd things that happen. However, any building that dates back to 1853, and especially one that has had a checkered past like this one, is bound to be creepy!

THE SPOON BEGINS TO BEND!

These two e-mails come courtesy of Marcello Truzzi, a noted sociologist who has a special interest in the principles of conjuring and the history of stage magic. The e-mails refer to the visit to Toronto made by Uri Geller, the controversial Israeli-born psychic who single-handedly made "spoon-bending" a household phrase.

The first e-mail was written by Allan Slaight, the broadcasting executive and publisher of books that illustrate the contributions of Stewart James, the postman of Courtright, Ontario, who was incredibly inventive when it came to originating magical effects. The letter is dated January 28, 2000.

The second e-mail came from David Ben, a lawyer and a noted magician, who (with director Patrick Watson) devised a successful "period" magic act that was premiered as part of the Stratford Festival.

Slaight and Ben are very observant people. I would not try to bend a spoon in their presence! In their e-mails they refer to Ray Hyman, the psychologist and noted skeptic, as well as to various other personalities familiar to illusionists and skeptics.

1. Allan Slaight

Hold me responsible for "this premature attempt to make a miracle out of nothing."

I've been in magic since 1939. I've toured in western Canada with an evening show of magic and mindreading. I immodestly state that I came across as a real psychic with uncanny powers. I wrote, with Howard Lyons, *Stewart James in Print*, and am now finishing up, with the invaluable assistance of Max Maven, a ten-year, two-volume effort called *The James File*, which will run to more than 1,600 pages.

I scoffed at those early Geller reports. I was 100% on Randi's side. I watched Geller blow his brains out on the Johnny Carson show. Then I forgot all about the guy until Marcello e-mailed me in mid October and suggested I might like to meet Uri, who was in Toronto on a publicity tour for his *Mind Medicine* book. I contacted him at his hotel, and arrangements were made to pick him up at noon on Saturday, October 16.

The two of us are in my car. After a very brief "nice to meet you," he immediately pulled a coffee spoon from his pocket. I am instantly suspicious. "It's from the hotel," he says. "Please make sure it's normal." I take the spoon and test it for any type of pre-weakening. Nothing. Solid as can be. It would have taken a considerable, two-handed effort to bend that particular spoon.

As I watch carefully (stare is a better word), Uri takes the spoon back. No switch. He holds the bowl between the forefinger and thumb of his left hand. Thumb underneath and the finger inside the bowl. He GENTLY strokes the spoon with the first two fingers of his right hand. No effort. No exertion. No tensing of muscles. Just a very soft caress of the handle of the spoon.

Before my eyes, the spoon begins to bend! It seems to DROOP. It bends not quite 45 degrees. He puts the spoon on the dashboard of my car and sits back in the passenger seat. The effing spoon continues to bend. He picks it up and hands it straight to me. It is now bent to right angles — 90 degrees. The metal is cold. Uri signs the spoon and gives it to me. (And all of this is reported to Marcello.)

Weirdly, and for reasons I now can't explain because for years I had lost all interest in Geller, I had ordered the Margolis book and it arrived the day before I met Uri. Prior to that incident in my car — which I reported that evening to a number of people including magicians David Ben, Daniel Zuckerbrot and Mark Mitton — I was not aware that there were "after-effect bending" reports. When I raced through the Margolis book the following day, I was staggered to encounter the part where a Margolis-owned spoon bends somewhat, is placed on the author's 14-year-old son's hand, then continues to bend.

That same Saturday evening, Geller joined some of us at a fund raiser for The Children's Own Museum, a cause dear to the heart of David Ben and his wife. David will receive this letter. I urge him to write up his account of a second spoon bending incident and forward it to this group.

Ray, I was the world's toughest skeptic until that bloody spoon bent before my eyes. I know the magician's methods — or most of them — and I have books and videos on spoon and key bending. What I witnessed is well beyond all that!

You have done a dandy job, from your vantage point, in airily dismissing my account, and those of others. You write: "… the question of scientific interest is not how many people claim to have 'seen' the item continue to bend but whether it did indeed continue to bend without physical contact."

The spoon now in my possession sure as hell did!

I agree with your commentary that Uri has had 30 years to prove his powers via photos or video and has not done so.

And you rightly point out that, as an amateur magician, I am not exempted from "the human equation."

Mind you, I thought you were doing just fine until you cited those first five examples. I would have quit when I was ahead — or at least not behind!

It would be nice to meet you sometime. Your one-man parade in the "Linking Ring" those many years ago was one of the very best.

Allan Slaight

2. David Ben

To Whom It May Concern:

I was one of the magicians Ray Hyman alluded to in his extensive missive regarding Uri Geller and the bending spoon. I too witnessed Geller bending a spoon. Soon after it occurred Marcello Truzzi asked me to describe what took place in more detail. The bending took place at a Gala dinner that I was hosting for the Children's Own Museum in Toronto. Here is the body of my letter to Marcello.

Here is what happened to the best of my recollection. I introduced and invited Geller to come to the stage to address the audience. I wasn't sure whether he would perform or just tell a few stories. He said he would do 3 minutes and then leave because he had to get to a radio interview via telephone to a U.S. station.

I introduce Geller. He tells a charming story about when he first recognized his powers. VERY SELF-EFFACING. Charming. Said with a "I can't believe it is true because it is so trivial" posture that he first became famous for bending spoons.

He asked everyone (450 people) to pick up their spoons. (It was a black tie gala dinner.) I gave him a hand-held microphone but it apparently wasn't working properly. He started to speak from the podium but moved into the audience. I got the microphone to work and followed him into the audience with the microphone directly under his mouth at all times. I was always standing to his right side. We moved from table to table.

I am unclear on the next point because it happened so fast. Initially I seem to recall that he picked up a spoon from the table. (He may have had it on his person but my recollection is that he picked it up from the table.) He kept on apologizing to say that it may or may not work. Imagine a large dance floor jutting out into the space with tables situated on three sides with the stage area for the band bordering one side. He picks up the spoon from the stage left side of the dance floor. Holds it in his left hand — high — my side. We sweep past the table bordering the left side and downstage sides of the dance floor. He holds the spoon by his fingertips to the right. Can't recall if he moved his right fingers over the arm of the spoon or just held the spoon with his left fingers.

Commented that sometimes the spoon will bend. I see a slow movement of the arm of the spoon. NOT 90 DEGREES. He gracefully shows the spoon to a variety of people stating, "Look ... you can see that it is bending."

We back-peddle to the stage left side of the band's stage where the lectern is located. He comments he will offer the spoon for auction as a fundraiser for the children's museum. Plants the seed that another spoon he bent sold for $25,000 at an auction in N.Y.C.

He takes out a pen and signs and dates the spoon. He comments that at times the spoon has continued to bend even after he has gone but that it ALWAYS stops (he can't explain it) at a 90 degree angle. He says that he will leave the spoon on the lectern where it may continue to bend. I am standing to the left of the lectern and he is standing to the left of me.

He reaches over to place the spoon on the lectern. It slides off because of the incline for speaker's notes. He picks it up and gently places over the moldling at the top of the lectern. It is balanced precariously. It does not appear to be at a 90 degree angle at this time. (I made a mental note of this because Slaight had already tipped me to the dashboard episode. I wanted to see if it really bent any further.) It did not appear to be 90 degrees when he placed it on the lectern.

He departs (from my left as I am in between him and the lectern and the spoon). I take the hand held mike and thank him on behalf of the audience. He departs to large applause. I immediately pick up the spoon from the lectern and place it into my pocket so that no one can steal it before I have the opportunity to auction it off. I notice that it is now at a perfect 90 degree angle — a different physical appearance than what I recall seeing when he placed it gently down on the lectern. I secretly shake my head because it is now different and I did not see him do one thing that was suspicious, with speed, without grace or charm. It was flawless. I have no idea what he did.

I now have the spoon at my home. It is perfect. I have seen many spoons bent by so-called experts. Uri is in a league of his own. The curvature of the bend is beautiful — not forced. I have said to many people that the curvature reminds me of a single line drawn by Matisse. It is a work of art. You can tell that it was created by a master. Quite wonderful. And he is a very gracious guest, and quite charming. I would open my home to him and his brother in law at any time.

What is even more interesting, however, is our conversation about David Blaine and David's posturing for the media. I thought that his comments, more than anything, raised doubts about any particular powers he may have professed to possess. Geller was very approachable, humane and wink, wink, wonderfully ambiguous.

I'm a fan.

Now, I would like to add a few further comments. Although I am not an expert in the paranormal, I am an expert in sleight of hand. I would stack up my knowledge and ability in sleight of hand against anyone in the world. I do not believe that Geller used sleight of hand to bend the spoon. (I have seen most of the spoon bending experts created by the magic community and their work is not very elegant when compared with Geller.)

Further, with no disrespect to Mr. Hyman, I find the explanation of the shift in focus to account for the visible bending of the spoon to be rather simplistic. I was briefed earlier in the day to watch for this should Geller attempt to bend a spoon. It was not at 90 degrees when it was placed on lectern. It was at 90 degrees afterwards.

You can probably sense from the tone of my letter to Marcello that I am not convinced that Geller has paranormal powers. I am rather indifferent. He may or may not. I am not prepared to state that he is a genuine psychic just because he performed something that I cannot explain. It was just a beautiful performance.

I do find, however, the actions of most skeptics repugnant. They seem such a rude and ungracious bunch. I would not want to perform for them even if I had psychic powers. I have certainly turned down well-paying work because the potential client was obnoxious. I would not blame Geller for doing the same.

David Ben

THE HAUNTED GUITAR

I receive a good number of strange stories over the phone, by fax, in the post, and now in e-mail form. The following story, one of the strangest of stories, came to me through the good auspices of Matthew Didier, who established the Toronto Ghosts and Hauntings Research Society on the Internet.

The communication comes from Patrick Cross, who identifies himself as a "ghost-hunter" based in Burlington, Ontario.

Here is the information that I received from him in May 2000. I subsequently met Patrick Cross at the second anniversary celebration of the Toronto Ghosts and Hauntings Research Society meeting at haunted Old Fort York on October 21, 2000. He is a native of Rexdale, Ontario, having grown up in a house with a background that lends itself to poltergeist-like activity. He has produced a cassette called *The Official Ghosthunter's CD* (Sci-Fi Productions Ltd.).

The Haunted Guitar

Patrick Cross

The following is the story that went on with the "Haunted Guitar"-Flying V!, submitted by Patrick Cross. He writes, "I am a member of the TGHRS (Toronto Ghosts and Hauntings Research Society) ... I have done many ghost investigations in haunted places and private residences."

Thanks go out to Eugena Macer-Story, a gifted spiritualist, for contacting the spirit entity of Patrick Cross's "Devil Guitar" The Flying V! at the X-Zone Symposium, May 16, 1999. Patrick found out that this guitar had a living evil or devil entity attached to it, which explained many problems that Patrick was having personally with a ghost presence!

After a two-hour psychic talk with the "spirit," Eugena suggested the guitar be destroyed or re-blessed to change the evil it was generating. It had a controlling effect on Patrick and anyone who touched or felt it. It would de-tune itself when played and would not allow anyone to play up-tempo music on it!

Also the guitar had been exposed to a ghost presence in a haunted house which left "ectoplasm" crystal residue on it. On the advice of Eugena, Patrick did destroy the guitar on Sunday night, May 16th, by taking it to a remote park, putting it in a steel garbage can and dousing it with gasoline and lighter fluid. Before lighting the guitar aflame, Patrick put a circle of salt around the container to stop the entity from escaping or attaching itself somewhere else. Patrick recited the Lord's Prayer three times and told the entity to go back to its source! It took a while to light the fire and a while to get the guitar to burn. Obviously, the entity did not want to be destroyed! Finally, after an hour, the Eye of the Condor guitar was completely charred and burnt to a crisp!

Let's hope the entity was destroyed and that it cannot haunt or possess anything else! The reason for all this was that the guitar had a spirit-hex on it, with one of the most powerful of all black gods, "EXU God," pronounced "Echu." So Patrick didn't want to be around this spirit or have any more bad experiences! Thanks to Eugena for the spirit cleansing and contacting this Spanish-speaking "very powerful spirit entity" which caused many bad things to happen with the destructive aura it sent out!

Eugena can be contacted at: 212-727-0002 in New York for spirit contact and cleansing.

Added Notes: The haunted guitar was purchased in a music store in Oakville, Ontario, second hand. Its history is interesting, since it came from Detroit, Michigan, and had been in a previous bar-restaurant fire, where everything was burned and destroyed except the guitar!

The guitar could not be played and would de-tune itself when anyone would try to play it except for songs of bad or loud negative music such as "heavy metal" or aggressive rock songs with death and destruction meanings. The guitar particularly liked one song I wrote and played, titled "Something Is Out There," which is about ghosts and evil entities and fear of the unknown with a heavy *X-Files* type edge. This was one of the very few songs the guitar would stay in tune with.

It had a very evil or bad aura around it, a three-foot aura, and at the X-Zone Symposium with Rob McConnell on the May 16th weekend 1999, after being taken out of its case and left standing up by my table, glasses around it started shattering, including the lighting going on and off in the conference room.

There were four witnesses to this, who all saw this happen as Rob walked in and said, "Get that thing back in its case and out of here! I don't need any more destructive energy from it!"

Case in point, I brought the guitar to the X-Zone Symposium to find out if it was causing all my bad luck, health and money problems at the time, and this was confirmed by Eugena Macer and the white witch of Niagara, Lady Ashley.

Also to note that on the weekend of the X-Zone Symposium, a major highway accident blocked all traffic from going to Niagara for 8 hours and also another multi-vehicle accident from the Canadian border blocked all traffic going towards St. Catharines and Toronto. It was a very paranormal weekend, as the X-Zone only had maybe 125 people out for 3 days! Very poor attendance, which normally would have generated some 3,500 people. Blame it on the events and the guitar, as Eugena Macer pointed out!

If you need any more information, I would be glad to tell you more about the guitar and I also have a video segment on YTV of another haunted guitar filmed in June 1999 and aired in March of this year on YTV Television with it talking!

Anyways, that's the documented story of the Haunted Guitar! Submitted for your consideration and review.

Thanks again,
Sincerely,
Patrick Cross
Ghosthunter and Leader of Canada's
Only Haunted Rock Band!

HERE'S THE SCOOP

Jack Kohane is a freelance photographer and writer who travels a lot around Ontario. He specializes in writing travel stories for newspapers about hotels, inns, and bed-and-breakfast establishments. He has spent a number of nights in strange bedrooms!

On August 31, 2000, he sent me an e-mail that said, "I'm continuing my travels to inns and B&Bs around Ontario … I came across this story at the Trinity House Inn in Gananoque."

Thanks, Jack, for the story. It comes from Brad Garside, proprietor of Trinity House Inn.

Here's the Scoop

Brad Garside

Have we got a TRUE story for you. This series of events happened for several years within the Inn from 1989 until about 1994.

We have been reluctant to say much about it because we don't want to name names and get the family upset, who still live in town, but we have PROOF. I'll fill you in on some of the bizarre details later but in a nutshell here's the scoop.

Many unusual things happening in the same room, a bathroom (not yours); renovation not going well, marble facings smashed to floor when plumbers installing, antique toilet smashed when Jacques stepped on lid before installation, floor tiles slid mysteriously up wall before bathroom completion; newlyweds with nightmares of someone being in the room and tearing down the drapes to jump out the window; strange clicking noises heard from the main floor above the bar in same location of activity on second floor; one of the children of the house (now in his 60's) returned to the house for a tour ... he froze at the door to the bathroom: "Father would have been very distressed." When asked why he said that, he explained, "He was very proud of his modern bathroom and you have put in these old fixtures which he did not like"; etc., etc.

Around 1991 we had a journalist staying with us. She wrote NON-fictional stories about the paranormal. We told her our story. She took a picture of the bathroom in question with a special high-speed film and said she would consult with a psychic. A YEAR later she returned to the Inn to drop it off. Mysteriously the negative had disappeared from her lab so she couldn't reproduce it. The face of a man appears in the tub. The profile of the face matches the only picture left in the house when we bought it. On the day that this man's brother died (who lived a couple of doors away) all activity stopped.

And yes we have the picture still with us to prove it! And yes, the ghost is no longer with us.

The house also shares the history of a Chinese princess who apparently the family did not like.

Another journalist came to write a story on her and the only one who could provide information was our man's brother, who had just died. We had complaints for years from housekeeping staff of cleaning a particular bathroom and when they would return to inspect before leaving for the day they would find long black hairs in the same area.

Then there's the story of the "Woman in White" that happened one evening in the dining room in front of a table of eight men.

There are many stories in town; however, the last one written about one of our neighbour's ghosts caused considerable emotions about letting "dead dogs lie."

Talk to you later.

Regards,
Brad Garside

TWO EXPERIENCES THAT CAN BE
CALLED PARANORMAL

"Lee," a correspondent unknown to me, sent me an e-mail in which he alluded to some unusual experiences that had befallen him. I encouraged him to write them down, or "write them up," as the idiom goes, and share these experiences with me and eventually with my readers.

He did so. I have edited them ever so slightly and, with his permission, have reproduced them here for your approval.

When I asked him to send me some details about himself, his life, and his experiences, he sent me the following information by e-mail on November 8, 2000:

> I'm 28 years old, now residing in Alberta, as you know, and I'm currently employed by an industrial manufacturing firm. I my spare time I'm a musician, a composer, and an artist. At this point in time, I'm also trying to become more computer literate, so as to enter the new millennium with both feet. I'm usually very busy. In the New Year, I plan on attending school to get a degree in graphic design. Since the aforementioned incidents occurred, I have also had a peripheral fascination with the paranormal.
>
> I realize that the stories that I have sent to you are far less dramatic than some of the ones I've read in your books. But I had never really encountered anything on a paranormal level before this, and it really made me think about things from a different viewpoint.
>
> I also should've mentioned that I'm a little bit leery about using my name to relate these stories,

because I wouldn't want it to get back to "Lynn" somehow that I was kind of airing out our dirty laundry. The reasons I have are also emotional, but I don't really know if I know how to put it into words.

Once again, thank you for taking the time out to read my stories. I hope that I somehow conveyed the incidents as they occurred. If you need any additional information, feel free to e-mail me at your discretion.

Thanks.

Two Experiences That Can Be Called Paranormal

"Lee"

Nov. 6, 2000
Dear Mr. Colombo,

Thank you for your response.

Where to begin? ...

First of all, I've only had two experiences that can be called paranormal.

1.

The first one that I'll tell you about isn't really what I'd call a regular "ghost story." But it had such a profound effect on me. I have to omit some of the details out of respect for some of the other people involved, and because some of this story may reflect badly on myself and others involved.

Let me give you some background.

As you know, I currently reside in Edmonton. I moved here roughly two years ago from Thunder Bay, Ontario. If you've never been there, it's a beautiful little city. You can drive for fifteen minutes out of town in any direction, and it's like being in a beer commercial; cliffs to jump off of into swimming holes, etc.

In any case, I had just moved into an apartment with a beautiful girl whom I'll call Lynn. She was already living there when we started dating, and she had told me that the place was "spooked." I don't know if I believed her or not, but I did know that the apartments DID have a bit of a history.

I wasn't there long when small things began to happen. For instance, we had a clock radio that would turn on sporadically. I thought it might be a power surge or something, but the switch to turn it on was manual, and would be clicked into the on position. Once when it happened, the song "Love Gun" by the band KISS happened to be playing. I remember making a joke that whatever it was it had good taste in music!

Lynn, who had lost a brother to suicide the year previous, seemed to think that it was a sign that he came in occasionally to check things out, or whatever ghosts do. I, however, do not think it was him, simply because his death occurred in British Columbia, and also because there had recently been a murder in the parking lot of our building.

At any rate, it was small things at first — the radio, the television going on by itself, things going missing. Then things began to get more pronounced. Lynn had a son from a previous relationship. He began talking to someone whom we couldn't see. I know that this is normal behavior for a child of his age, about two and a half years, but there was something rather creepy about it; it gave both of us chills. Well, it gave me chills, anyway. Lynn was still under the impression that it was her brother visiting.

One Saturday morning, for some reason, Lynn and her son had mercifully let me sleep in. I had wakened at about 10:00 a.m., and sauntered into the living room just wearing my jeans. I sat down on the arm of the couch and watched her son play with his toy trucks while I was waiting for some coffee to brew.

Suddenly (this part is a little difficult to explain, I'm not even sure I understand), I felt as if there was a presence coming down the hall towards me. I felt as if someone had taken a bucket of static electricity, as if it were water, and thrown it on me. It happened in about two seconds, and the hair on one side of my head was sticking out. (I wear my hair really long, by the way.) Even though I said nothing, Lynn's son was looking up at me incredulously, almost as if to say, "He's talking to you." For at least a minute after, you could hear the crackling of static in the room.

At this point I really started to take full notice of what Lynn had been telling me. We had a ghost.

Shortly after, we were sitting down in the kitchen one night after her son had gone to bed, and she began to tell me about some of the strange dreams that she had been having. Now, I don't know if I'm that suggestible, but that very night I had the weirdest dream that I've ever had. It was very vivid, but it didn't come back to me until the following evening. It had to do with all three of us being awakened in the middle of the night in a panic, and rushing out of the apartment for some reason. The dream stayed with me for the rest of the time I was living there.

Another time, I was getting ready to take a shower, when I heard a peculiar noise in the bathroom. When I looked up, the square cardboard tiles of our ceiling were being pushed up simultaneously! I didn't get a sense of fear as I watched this as much as I did a sense of fascination. I couldn't believe what I was seeing! I had my shower and by the time I got out, the phenomenon had dissipated.

One of the last major incidents in the apartment happened one night when I got up to use the facilities. I don't know what time it was and I was half asleep at the time. After I had used the washroom, I had intended to go into the kitchen to have a cigarette. As I started down the hallway, I was startled by a figure that I can only explain in terms of a shadow coming towards me.

Immediately I thought that Lynn had gotten up as well and didn't see me walking towards her in the dark. Instinctively I put my hands out to brace her from bumping into me. The figure went right through me, or vice versa! I was so cold afterwards, that I sat in a hot bath for nearly an hour, trying to get warm.

As I said, I've omitted some of the details from this story because of some of the things that happened in our relationship after the fact. The relationship itself was more traumatic than any haunting ever could be. Lynn ended up doing some things to me that I just can't forgive her for. But to this day I miss her and her son greatly.

2.

The next story that I'll share with you happened to me about a year later.

My interest was piqued in the whole subject of ghosts and hauntings. One night, over drinks, with a couple friends, I discussed this subject. We had already made plans to go camping the following weekend at a place that had a rather bad reputation for ominous and malevolent phenomena. To be honest, I don't know the history of the area. I just took all the rumours I had heard at face value.

Rather foolishly, we brought a Ouija board with us. I've never heard anything good about the consequences of using one. We were all in for a little more than we bargained for.

There were between twelve and fourteen of us. The first night that we were there, we had more or less succumbed to just listening to loud music and drinking by the campfire. The thoughts of ghosts and such things were the furthest things from our minds collectively. The next evening we had gone into town to get some firewood (as we weren't allowed to take any from the surrounding area).

Just after we had gotten back, a friend of mine saw the Ouija board sitting in the trunk of his car from the previous weekend. At first we all kinda laughed about it. Then after a few drinks, it was out on the hood of the car. Although I wasn't actively participating with this, I was a little bit unnerved. There was — and I'm not sure that I have the proper vocabulary to describe this — there was just a strange sensation, and I wasn't the only one who noticed it.

As it began to get dark (I'm not trying to be overly dramatic, just cataloguing the events as I recall them), we heard what sounded like voices coming from the bushes off in the distance. I had already had a few drinks, so I can't claim to be the first person who noticed them. After a while they died off, and we continued partying; business as usual. However, we were all startled, to say the least, when a horrid screaming started to come from the forest area. It sounded like a woman, a female who was either scared half to death or was being raped or something. Whatever it was, it sounded foul.

If we were more sober that night, I'm sure that we would've left. Instead, we were convinced that there WAS someone in trouble, and we turned all of our vehicles towards the bushes with the headlights on high. Some of us began to put two and two together: the area's bad reputation, the Ouija board, the sounds and sensations that we had been hearing all night. Then we began to get a little nervous! After a short while, things began to get a little more intense. In the forest — very near us, I might add — we could hear something of immense proportions moving though the woods at a great rate of speed, all around us.

This is pretty much where the story ends, unfortunately (or fortunately). The sound that we heard eventually moved off. I can't say for certain that what we heard wasn't an animal of some sort; I'd be a fool to not to consider that possibility. However, the sensations that we all felt, along with what we ALL heard, led us to the consensus that what we were witnesses to that night was something of a paranormal and unpleasant nature.

On that note, I hope you enjoy these stories. I can only assure you that they are true and that they happened the way that I remember them. With that, I'll just finish by saying, "Submitted for your approval."

ACTUAL EVENTS

This letter offers the reader a passel of experiences. (The experiences are eerie, to be sure!)

The letter originated as an e-mail, which I received on January 17, 2001. I am grateful to the correspondent, Susan George, who makes her home in Wiarton, Ontario.

I wondered if she came from a Welsh background. So in subsequent correspondence, conducted the following month, I asked her about this, and she replied as follows:

"I am 'Heinz 57' Canadian: a little English, a little German, and a touch of Scots. I understand the Welsh are known for being superstitious and great believers in ghosts roaming castles."

What I should have asked Mrs. George is, "Are you Celtic?" The Scots, the Irish, the Welsh, the Cornish, and people from Brittany are all Celtics in background and felt to be deeply intuitive. The account that she wrote shows a degree of sensitivity that might well be described as Celtic, if not Welsh.

She further wrote, "My husband and I and our three children live on a hundred-acre farm outside of Wiarton. We are self-employed. I run a small horse-boarding facility. My daughter and I are the horse enthusiasts. We own quarter horses. My daughter rides a sixteen-year-old gelding, while I ride our three-year-old filly who was born on the farm.

"I have always worked in animal-related fields. Before moving to Wiarton, I ran a successful dog-grooming shop out of my home and bred boxer dogs.

"I love the area of the Bruce Peninsula and have painted scenes in acrylic of the rugged escarpment of Georgian Bay and Lake Huron.

"I have had my poetry published in an anthology and received an editor's choice award.

"I had developed an interest in the metaphysical world, paranormal, and the supernatural, due to strange occurrences that gradually caught my attention.

"I do not consider myself psychic at all, although I am intuitive and I believe I have precognitive capabilities which I had discovered through years of dream journaling."

Actual Events

Susan George

January 16, 2001

Attention: Mr. John Robert Colombo

I have recently read and enjoyed your book *Ghost Stories of Canada*. After having read many ghostly accounts and after experiencing some strange happenings, I feel comfortable sharing with you a few of the following interesting experiences. I do not refer to these experiences as "stories" because they were actual events that involved one or more of my basic five senses. I believe these events to have been quite real. Having witnesses on occasions helps reinforce the experience to be quite real.

In the early 1990s, my husband and I were undertaking major renovations of our storey-and-a-half, pink Mansfield-sided wartime house. The house is located the south side of Paris, Ont., in a subdivision originally set aside in the 1940s for returning WWII soldiers.

The event that I am about to tell about is the most puzzling and the creepiest. My husband was very much the sceptic when it came to belief in ghostly phenomena — until this experience occurred.

I had gone to use our washroom facility when I lifted the seatcover to the toilet and saw and felt steam rise from the toilet bowl. I stood dumbfounded. I called for my husband to check it out. He came into the washroom and examined the condensation on the inside of the toilet seat lid. He then removed the lid of the toilet tank to discover that the water in the tank was steaming hot! He was puzzled and he suggested that we ask a plumber to check it out. We were going to call a plumber for some other work that needed to be done anyway. The plumber came to do the other work and examined the tank to find that the water was cold, not steaming hot. He said with assurance that it was impossible for hot water to fill the toilet since toilets are only plumbed to cold waterlines. Yet on two occasions we had discovered steaming hot water in the tank.

The morning of May 15, 1992, I awoke from a vivid dream that left me with a racing heartbeat and the thought of my grandmother. The dream left me with negative feelings. In the dream I saw my father transform from a baby, through the stages of growth, all the way to adulthood. I didn't see my grandma, however, though she was very much present and I sensed her adoration for my dad. Later that morning I journaled this dream, and sad feelings clung to me throughout the day. Later that day, I received a phone call from my mother telling me that grandma had died. I didn't feel shocked.

Not too long after the experience with grandma, several disturbances happened. I ignored them. Half-heartedly we would joke, saying that a dead relative came to visit. I began taking more notice when I awoke from a dead sleep (no pun intended!), having heard the brass doorknob spring back after being turned. It seemed the bedroom door was being opened, maybe by one of my children. I looked. No one was in the room and the door was still closed.

I got up, thinking that one of the kids needed me. All three of my children were sound asleep in their beds. At the time my husband was out of the country on a business trip. I am not sure how much time passed, but another night I was awakened by a persistent buzzing. I got out of bed to investigate and I found the cause to be the malfunctioning of my microwave oven. I unplugged it and went back to bed. Over the next few weeks, my husband and I had to remember to keep unplugging the microwave when it was not in use until we could arrange to have a technician look at it. The Sears repairman suggested that the microwave had a cracked computer panel. It was possible, I guess. However, we had had it for years and we hadn't dropped it. The repairman said it was safe to use but that we should unplug it after each use if I wanted to continue to use it until it could be replaced. After a while it stopped buzzing so we forgot to unplug it. Time passed and I was reminded of the strange problem when some friends were discussing spooky happenings. I told them about the buzzing microwave. Later that day the microwave started buzzing again soon. Then we moved and it did not act up for the next two-and-a-half years. Lightning destroyed the microwave.

If the above pesky happenings were grandma's way of saying "Hi!" we have since visited in my dreams. This has left me feeling in my awake state very happy.

The first time I sighted an apparition, I had two witnesses!

In the winter of 1999, my husband was away on a business trip in Portugal. To our new home on a secluded farm in Wiarton, Ont., I had invited two new girlfriends for a "girls' night." We were enjoying chatting while drinking wine. Our livingroom and kitchen are open concept, with cathedral ceiling. For light, I had many candles and lamps burning, and outside, our raised, ranch-style house, with its massive veranda, was lit up with porch lights. We sat on a comfy sectional couch. Kathy sat at the far side of the couch, while Donna sat in the very corner adjoining the sectional, and I sat next to Donna on the opposite end of the couch to Kathy, when I saw it walk pass the window behind Donna and me on the couch. I didn't dare mention what I saw to my new friends. I didn't want to jeopardize new friendships! I saw Kathy's eyes widen. Donna and Kathy simultaneously asked in surprise, "Did you see that?"

My reply was, "Yes!"

The three of us jumped up and faced the window, repeating what we thought we saw, when the shadow walked by two more times! There was no mistaking the shadowy form of a person. We blew out the candles and flipped on all the lights in the house. It was 1:00 a.m. when it came time for Donna to leave to go home. Kathy and I walked out to Donna's vehicle. Kathy and I proceeded to check the front steps and veranda for footprints of a Peepin' Tom. We found undisturbed snow that drifted from the steps to the veranda flooring.

If you find the above interesting and have questions or desire questions to be answered I would be delighted to assist someone who can relate to similar experiences.

Sincerely,
Susan George

EVERYONE FOUND THE PLACE ENCHANTING

Charlotte Fielden Morris is a wise woman of many talents and abilities. As a mime, she studied under the redoubtable Marcel Marceau. As an actress, she played a leading role in an early production of the Stratford Festival. As an author, she wrote a compelling autobiographical novel. As a playwright, she has seen many of her scripts staged. As a therapist, she has helped people for more than two decades. All in all, she is personable, resourceful, adaptable, beautiful, and probably a little psychic.

On January 31, 2001, Charlotte sent me what she calls this "anecdote." I call an account like this a memorate. It is simply a spirited account of an experience that leaves her (and the reader) wondering what it was all about to this day.

The reader will appreciate the fact that Timothy Findley is the widely published novelist and former actor who until the 1990s lived in a farmhouse outside Cannington, northeast of Toronto.

She signed her account "Bo Peep," a pet name based on the fact that the last time I set eyes on Charlotte Fielden Morris it was in a Toronto supermarket and her head was framed by long braids and she looked like no one else but Little Bo Peep!

Everyone Found the Place Enchanting

Charlotte Fielden Morris

Hi JR, here's the anecdote as promised. I hope you like it, Bo Peep.

In the late '70s, when I was an active and founding member of the Writers Union of Canada, I had the good fortune of living out one of my fantasies. I had always dreamed of living on a farm. When my family was grown and my marriage over, I left Montreal and resumed my residency in Ontario. Through the Union's grapevine I learned that Timothy Findley was renting out a farm in Cannington. I was fortunate to be his new tenant. There was something magical about the place, except for the cluster flies, but that's another story! From the very first day I felt a presence, and learned that the Georgian farmhouse was originally the manse for the local minister. I used only a portion of the large house except when I had frequent guests. Everyone found the place enchanting. It proved to be enchanted as well as enchanting. It was the last evening in the farmhouse. All my belongings, except for the two large, heavy speakers for my stereo unit, were packed for my move to Toronto. I was going full circle, back to the city where I was born and grew up. My best friend in Cannington — also a writer and member of the Union — and her naturalist husband came from the village to help me pack the speakers. They brought a picnic basket with a delicious "last supper," complete with knife, fork, and gingham serviette. The speakers stood waiting in two corners of the room I had used as my writing studio. A large window, still with its original bubble glass, overlooked the north pasture where Timothy's two horses, Sandy, the workhorse, and Flicka, the quarter horse he had allowed me to ride, were grazing to their hearts' content in the north pasture. Just as we were about to lift the speakers into the packing crates, in a voice that seemed to boom out of the speakers, in a voice definitely not mine, a voice more a man's than a woman's — I begin to sing:

> Oh God our help in ages past,
> Our hope for years to come,
> Our shelter from the stormy blast
> And our eternal home.

I belted out the hymn in perfect pitch, tune, and words. I never knew the words to that hymn and still don't. I remembered the tune enough to call a friend and get the words to it to tell this story. All three of us in that room shivered and developed serious goosebumps. Even though my friend's scientist husband pooh-poohed it, there was no doubt in my mind that the ghost of the minister long past had come to say good-bye and send me on my way with his blessing! Believe it or not — I did.

ASTRAL TRAVELLING

Charlotte Fielden has been a family friend for more years than my wife Ruth and I care to count. I always associate Charlotte with Montreal, where we would visit her, but truth to tell, she is a native of Toronto and she has spent the last two decades living in her native city, where she teaches relaxation techniques and offers past-life regressions.

Here is an account of some of her astral travels. Charlotte mentions the late Marcel Vogel. If you check his name through Google.com on the Internet, you will learn more about him. He was one of those Renaissance personalities who made contributions to science and technology, on the earthly plane, and to consciousness studies, on the astral plane.

Astral Travelling

Charlotte Fielden Morris

When I was a child I flew in many of my dreams, at times to escape the monsters that lurked in the night, at times for the sheer pleasure of it. It was therefore no surprise to me when later in life during my exploration of psychic phenomena with Ouija boards and time-travel into past lives, that I would be drawn to and successful at astral travelling.

My first adventure happened inadvertently when I was napping. Just before nodding off, one of my arms seemed to enter a parallel room, not unlike the one I was in, and startled, I quickly withdrew it. Feeling a little braver because I saw that I could control whatever was happening to me, I put in one arm, then the other, then one leg followed by the other, and *voilà*! I was elsewhere. I became proficient at taking off like Superman and travelling to anywhere in the world I wished to go. It was easier to do when I felt passionately about someone or something.

One of the objects of my affection was my collie Cokie. I was in Toronto the night he died, and he was in Montreal. I was half-awake when I was drawn up into my astral body, and flew at the speed of light over the cities between Cokie and me. What I thought at first were the bright street lamps on the end of silvery wavering poles turned out to be people sleeping and hovering above their physical bodies. Somehow I knew that, unquestionably. I reached Cokie just as he was dying and saw his long muzzle pointing upwards like a cone of light. It was an achingly moving reunion that allowed us to say good-bye.

Another astral journey I remember clearly was during a seminar I attended given by Marcel Vogel, a crystallographer at International Business Machines. He was with IBM for twenty-five years, and during those years developed a crystal that is still used in their computers. I found him to be a scientist searching for knowledge beyond the parameters of our three-dimensional world. Vogel had a lab at his disposal at IBM to do this sort of work, and experimented with plants. At the seminar he claimed that what we thought affected them as well as ourselves. According to Vogel, our thoughts could make us sick or make us well.

During the seminar I sat at the back of a crowded conference room, totally engaged by Vogel's manner and mind. At one point he wanted a volunteer to go on a journey through one of his crystals he used for thought projection. There were many volunteers, and I don't know how he saw me at the back of the room, but he pointed in my direction and said, "You!"

I looked around to see if he was speaking to someone near me, and he said, "No, you!"

Realizing he meant me, I made my way to the front of the room. I had an instant and total trust in Vogel. He invited me to sit down on a chair facing the audience, and I immediately sat in a comfortable lotus position. For some reason, I knew I would be there for a while. I closed my eyes. Just being near Vogel put me in an altered state. When he placed a small crystal in my hand and told me that he was taking me on a trip to where I have longed to go, I was out of the room in a flash, flying towards the Himalayas.

All through my journey, Vogel kept asking me questions like, "Where are you now?" "What do you see?" "What's happening?"

I replied to all his questions without hesitation. I described a great green lush valley, and in the background, the Himalayas glowing like molten gold in the sunset. I described the ancient temples, the lamaseries that would be destroyed, and in fact, no longer exist. I wanted to stay, to enter their silence, but Vogel called me back. I sat for a while without moving or speaking, my eyes still closed. Vogel's right hand rested on my left shoulder. I felt an infusion of warmth. He asked me what was happening, and I replied, "I am receiving a healing. The Buddha is here in a giant green crystal sending out healing energies to everyone in the room." There was a profound silence.

At the time, I believed it was the Buddha performing the healing, but with the passing of years, I am certain that it was Marcel Vogel sending his own loving thoughts to each of us.

ABOUT A HOUSE IN BARRIE

Out of the blue I received two e-mails from a young woman named Chrysta Rowland.

In the first e-mail, she asked if I was familiar with a house that she and her husband had once occupied. I e-mailed back and requested more particulars, as I was familiar with some houses in the vicinity that were said to be haunted, but not with the one to which she was referring. She wrote again to supply further particulars.

Here are the three e-mails, minimally copy-edited.

It would seem to me that Chrysta is, as she says she is, a natural-born "sensitive." It would further seem to me that the house in question — a good, menacing name for it would be Hunter House! — is a bad place to be.

Perhaps it is the haunt of a poltergeist, a series of disturbances.

About a House in Barrie

Chrysta Rowland

From: Chrysta Rowland
To: jrc@inforamp.net
Sent: Saturday, May 12, 2001 12:50 PM
Subject: Haunted houses in Ontario, referred by the Barrie Public Library

Hi, I recently inquired about a house in Barrie that I resided at for 5 years (5 years too long) and they responded with your name, etc. I'm sorry but I am not sure who you are or what help you could be to me. I understand that you have written some books on Ontario Hauntings

... I doubt that you would have covered this house but perhaps you could let me know the titles you have written.

I'm really trying to research the history of the house that I lived in for personal reasons ... perhaps they thought you could suggest ways of finding info out. All I can tell you is that I am a very "sensitive" person who has noticed at various places I have lived or stayed very odd goings on ... I went through horrid things at that residence and now have moved to a fresh new home with none of those problems!

Guests in the other house noticed things as well (even strangers). I believe the house was built for or by the "Hunters." It was Victorian. I was in an office here that had old newspaper clippings about a "Hunter" that had gone missing on the lake. I don't believe that is him who is disturbing the house now but possibly a relative.

I have now serious health problems from this and a family member of the owner prior to us had a death in the family from similar health issues, I believe.

There were far too numerous occurrences ... similar to the Amityville House ... that I feel I needed to share with others but my husband thinks I'm nuts. (I really think that he believes me and is not willing to admit.)

The finding of my new house was also as if I was being "guided" by a good force, as I really had no plans to go out that day and buy a house, especially with its bizarre coincidental location.

I really hope you can help me out. I haven't mentioned any of the "goings on" at the house because I want to make sure that any info I get is accurate. A couple of friends say they saw things in the house. I'm not sure if I believe them, as I had discussed my thoughts with them and they may have just imagined it. I never experienced what they "saw."

There could be a lot of coincidences, but I can't tell you how many can't seem to be explained and I have other people who experienced them with me. We all eventually thought each one was doing these things, but how?

I hope to hear back from you, if you know of anyone who could suggest explanations for "hauntings," please let me know.

Thank you for your time, bye for now,

Chrysta

To: "Chrysta Rowland"
Subject: Hi
Date: Sat, 12 May 2001 16:42:50 -0400

Dear Chrysta Rowland:

Check my homepage for information about my publications, including "Ghost Stories of Ontario," "Mysteries of Ontario," and "Mysterious Canada." The Barrie library should have copies of them or they will interloan them for you. The address of the homepage appears below.

Why not send me a detailed account of your experiences and I will tell you what I think about them, based on my reading and information. I can't tell whether I have information on your house unless I know where it is located!

John Robert Colombo

From: "Chrysta Rowland"
To: jrc@inforamp.net
Subject: Re: Hi, Nice hearing from you
Date: Wed, 16 May 2001 16:59:08 -0400

The house that I want info about is at 159 Owen Street, Barrie, Ontario.

I believe it was built for a family named Hunter; it is a Victorian home and is downtown. They may have had something to do with a newspaper way back; the library has not been of much help here.

Here is a list of some of the occurrences that happened while we were there.

Day 1, the evening we moved in, the boiler on a fairly new heating system blew. We were forced to replace it and had to stay for a week in the master bedroom as it was the only room with electric heat.

A few weeks after, I was watching a movie with a painter friend and my husband in the same room. All windows were closed when a freezing draft seemed to come out of nowhere. The painter and I both sensed it and looked at each other at the same moment. My husband didn't notice the draft.

The painter was cleaning out things from the attic and found a little old lady's hat collection, probably Victorian or 30's. He wanted to throw them away; I had a strange feeling and asked him to put them in the shed with some old pictures. We were never able to gain access as the shed locked and even the professional locksmith that came out was unable to get in. Eventually, I had to have someone cut a hole in the garage door to gain entry.

People who came to the housewarming said they felt very uncomfortable and that something was just not right about the house. I dismissed this. One person said they heard a small child crying. I didn't hear this, but if they did there was no way they could have heard something from outside as the house was as solid and sealed as a rock.

Things began to go "missing"; some things "turned up" and others didn't.

My husband and I fought CONTINUALLY. The fights were bizarre and seemed to be about nothing. They were mostly psychological nastiness and drinking became an issue. Looking back they were bizarre, out of control lunacy. Borderline the movie "War of the Roses" but for no reason. We don't have average couple's concerns.

Neither of us liked being in the master bedroom. Finally he fought so much in there with me I moved him into the room next door. The day I moved his things in we fought so bad he left and he had fought so hard to get out of the master bedroom I couldn't understand what was going on. I arranged for counselling for us that got nowhere. I was TERRIFIED for no reason to be in the room before bed. I'd be lucky if I got 3 hours sleep, always waking around 3 and awake until 7. There was physical violence between my husband and me from the fights in that room. Sometimes the t.v. would appear to be lit up glowing as if on, but it was off.

Halloween eve; I had two friends sleep over, I had said goodnight and was heading to my room when a LIVE BAT flew at me down the hall. My husband didn't believe me but my friends got it out of the house and verified what happened.

I had moved there for fresh air ... the old oil tank under the drive spilled into the basement causing the house to be severely polluted. It

169

took 5 years to try and clean up the problem. Basically moving was all we could do. We were unable to stay in the home and had money to get hotel rooms and stay at the cottage, but now we all have health problems.

Apparently the little girl who lived there prior died of lung problems as well.

We bought a dog; the dog REFUSED to come into the house and would sit by the back door waiting to get out. She was normal at the cottage and is at our new house as well.

The lights would go out periodically for no reason and if I picked up the phone to call anyone, when they went on, I could hear conversations clear as if they were in the house. Once in particular I heard a woman saying to a man that the police were all outside the library (that was down the street) and that there had been a bomb scare. The man answered that he would get his dog and go and see. I called my husband and told him not to drive that way home and called the police. The police said there was no such thing going on.

There were hundreds of little tiny flies similar to fruit flies that would come and go, usually if there was a conflict in the home at the time.

A snuff bottle collection that belonged to my grandmother that was contained in a locked cabinet seemed to have a life of its own. The bottles looked as if someone was taking them out and looking at them and setting them back down. This seemed to happen during the night. We tried making the cabinet vibrate to see if that was moving them and they didn't budge. Someone thought that maybe the heat and cold, being on an outside wall, might do it. They hang on a similar wall now and have never moved.

Because of the things going missing and some being found, my husband and I and one friend that was regularly over constantly blamed each other for doing it causing dreadful fights.

One cleaning lady quit after a summer alone there saying the house was haunted. She wouldn't say why she said that.

When preparing the house for the real estate lady, my bathtub filled up and overflowed while she was there I had been washing out sweaters, but was sure that it was off. It almost seeped through to the dining room ceiling.

My friend and I were taking loads of things to the new house and ARE POSITIVE we double checked locking the front door as these are things we both are nervous about. When I arrived back home I had a strange feeling to go and check yet again and it was wide open. I could have lost my husband's dog. We always entered from the back door and it was a 4,000 square foot home … we always double checked doors as the dog is tiny.

On my last night there I had another friend helping me and we were alone waiting for my husband; I asked him if he would go down to the basement with me to check that I had everything as I hadn't gone down in the basement for 4 years as I was afraid, though it was a large dry basement I didn't want to see the "oil problem" reminders. He gave me an odd look and I said, "Oh, don't worry, there's nothing down there that will hurt you"; we no sooner stepped of the last step when all the lights went out causing us to run.

I wonder what you think of these goings on; my husband, myself and the dog do not have any of these goings on at the new house. If anything we may have the odd argument but I find they are like flash-backs a Vietnam vet would have after the trauma we went through emotionally in the house.

I will also mention that typical of most haunting stories the house sat for a very long time on the market and the previous owner had to take a drastic reduction of the price. I sold quickly and took a loss, but my health has suffered greatly from living there. I'm just glad to be gone. I'm sure that my departed mother had something to do with my finding the present house as it is so hidden from anyone that no one knows it is here and it is also downtown. It amazingly enough is built next door to where my mother attended school as a child. I had no intention of looking at houses that day and now … It also has a bedroom already in my favourite colour, the windows I like, and the sink I wanted when I inherited mum's cottage but couldn't get it on order in time. It is in the middle of a forest and almost as if mum had "flown" over and picked it out to get me out of the other house. I think her worry over me at the other place made her ill as she always said she just couldn't believe the bad luck I was seeming to have.

I also forgot to mention that we had our car completely stripped while on vacation and even though it was parked in a secured location … I knew it was going to happen and my husband was white as a ghost that I had had this premonition.

I have always been sensitive to "ghosts" and have had many premonitions about usually bad things. My husband has witnessed these time after time. I will also mention that I was predicting things so much for awhile many years ago and sensing things that I sought a therapist who didn't seem to think I was crazy! I feel I have lived in 2 places on vacation that I had to leave as I felt bad things.

I had a room in an apartment in Toronto that I couldn't go into, though it was bright and sunny, and I know a friendly ghost was living at St. Clair and Yonge in my house there as we could hear him walking up the stairs at night. I just consider myself lucky to have noticed things at the other house and gotten out of there.

Anyhow, look forward to hearing from you again and reading some of your things.

Bye for now,
Chrysta

WRAPPED IN A 'BOW

Rainbows meet a multitude of needs. They move us emotionally. They intrigue us intellectually. They seem to symbolize gateways or pathways. *Somewhere over the rainbow ... There's a pot of gold at the end of the rainbow ... Rainbows in your eyes ...*

All of us are familiar with solar rainbows. But not everyone has ever seen a lunar 'bow; many don't even know about them and their eerie loveliness. This account describes one that was visible outside Truro, Nova Scotia, on September 5–6, 1998.

I first read this account, entitled "Wrapped in a 'Bow," in the journal *Parabola*, Summer 2001. My attention was caught by the Maritime locale, but the subject was of interest to me, and the loving treatment of the locale and subject are praiseworthy indeed. I wrote to the contributor, Thomas R. Birmingham, an American writer, and he agreed that I could share it with my readers.

Wrapped in a 'Bow

Thomas R. Birmingham

Our Saturn sedan was on a mini roller coaster ride, rising and falling, tilting and turning along the asphalt's double-yellow tracks, as we made haste toward our bed and breakfast in Truro, Nova Scotia. It was 8:30 p.m., and the western horizon had already become a portal for the sun's retreat. In exchange for this fiery deposit, a diffracted offering of indigo, emerald, yellow, and rose highlights was returned, foreshadowing a story of nature's supreme gift.

My wife, Amy, and I were celebrating our fifth wedding anniversary en route to see the famous "tidal bore" of Nova Scotia, and this particular evening held much promise and reflection for us. We had been told by several Halifaxians that Truro, which sits at the mouth of the Salmon River and acts as the headwater to the eastern reaches of the Bay of Fundy, provided ideal viewing for this natural phenomenon of water, gravity, and geology. The added bonus was the serendipitous timing of our arrival with that of the full moon. However, our conjugal celebration was tempered by the solemn reality that only seventy-five miles southwest of Truro, families, friends, and emergency workers were shrouded in grief and remorse caused by the recent crash of Swissair Flight 111 near Peggy's Cove.

I first heard about the famous, record-breaking tidal changes of the Bay of Fundy at my grandmother's feet. It was during family vacations at our summer home in Bar Harbor, Maine, that she etched in my mind's eye the power and wonder of the ocean. I remember Grandma turning a mundane, twice daily occurrence into a major phenomenon for the people and creatures depending on the sea for sustenance. After dinner she would walk my sister CCB and me down the dirt access road to the edge of Bar Island. We would often watch the *Bluenose II* glide slowly in and out from behind the Porcupine Islands on its return voyage from Nova Scotia. While exhausting whatever remaining energy we had left from the day, she filled our heads with images of how tides affect where mussels, barnacles, and seaweed grow. I related to these stories, because they were happening right before my eyes. I never forgot them.

Twenty years had passed, and as we prepared for our pilgrimage to Nova Scotia those images of the famous floods of salt water solidified our commitment to seeing this natural spectacle. So, upon arriving on the Scotia Prince ferry in Yarmouth, we put out our "traveller's sonar," sounding the locals, book stores, and newspapers for the best time and place to witness the return of the tide. Most of the talk and news was appropriately focused on the terrible tragedy of Flight 111, but we picked up enough details in Halifax to guide us northeast along Route 102 to Truro.

We arrived at the Stewart House B&B around 8:45 p.m. It was the closest place we could find to see the tidal bore, because most of the other available housing was either booked for the Labour Day weekend or set aside for rescue workers and families of the crash victims. We

quickly unpacked our car, went through the polite niceties involved
with intruding on someone's home, settled into our room, and pulled
together some warm clothes for a cool evening under the stars. The
local paper had a column devoted to the tidal bore, which stated that
is was due to arrive in Truro at exactly 12:17 AM. This gave us some
time for dinner and to scope out the viewing area.

The coastal village was small and the height of the tourist season
had passed, so we headed straight to the Palliser Restaurant. Our con-
tacts in Halifax told us this was the best place to see the bore, because
it provides public access to the river, picnic tables, strong lights for
nocturnal wave watching, and an information kiosk. It also has a
restaurant that stopped serving dinner at 8:30, so we poked around the
gift shop. The attendant assured us this was going to be a great night
to see the bore, and the lights would come on around 11:30. She also
encouraged us to visit the information kiosk, which was just across the
parking lot toward the river.

As we sauntered past the remaining cars in the lot, we noticed the
kiosk to our left. A dim light was shining from around the corner, so
we proceeded to the far side of the humble shack. The woman at the
gift shop told us to just go on in, so that was the plan. My pulse quick-
ened with anticipation, for it was here that I would finally witness my
first tidal bore, twenty-something years after Gertrude H. Driscoll first
whispered those stories in our ears.

The sting of salty air and smell of low tide were unmistakable as we
made our way toward the entrance. It took little effort to fill my lungs
with these natural emanations, because I faced directly into the south-
westerly wind, which was brisk and steady. Amy got a quick chill, so
she retreated inside the kiosk. I stood alone at the top of the hill, my
eyes slowly scanning the darkened horizon for the river. The mani-
cured lawn gently fell away from the parking lot and tables, and led to
a wide expanse of marsh cord grass. The scene before me was illumi-
nated by the full moon, which was playing hide and seek with the racing clouds. I guessed that the Salmon River basin was neatly tucked
below the slope, just out of sight, so I turned my gaze skyward.

It was then that I noticed before me an eerie, grey light suspended in
the night's sky. Being unfamiliar with these parts, I first wondered if it was

a weak spotlight advertising some new movie or car dealership, but this particular vapor was too delicate, too surreal to be man made. Then, as the wind unmasked the moon from behind the latest cloud, the muted grey became shimmering silver. This iridescent light embodied a mystical, enchanted quality that I had never seen before. Shortly, the faint silhouette became more defined in the brightening sky, and suddenly a massive arch erupted out of thin air. This manifestation spanned the autumnal stars, and possessed faint traces of indigo and emerald at the right base.

My poetic mind returned to the evening's earlier sunset, and then to the memory of the reflection of the "Gateway to the West" that I had once seen along the Mississippi River outside of St. Louis. However, my rational voice began to doubt what it saw. I rushed into the kiosk to find Amy reading about the tidal bore, and quickly hastened her outside to verify my observation. She, too, saw the muted colours above us, and was also struck by its fantastic beauty. We stood there quietly wondering what could have caused such a spectacle. Soon, the wind began throwing tiny water droplets at us, like needles of rain through the aberration, and I had my answer.

Before us was the nocturnal image of Iris, goddess of the rainbow. She was "running on the rainy wind," as Homer once said. My mind roared back to words from Arthur Zajonc's book, *Catching the Light: The Entwined History of Light and Mind*. My personal epiphany had a scientific explanation. I had spotted my first lunar rainbow.

Some of the greatest minds of human history have contemplated the cause of rainbows, including Aristotle, Descartes, and Newton. Explanations have ranged from the spiritual to the mundane. Today, we know that rainbows are a result of several natural phenomena working in elegant harmony. For example, the sequence of colours in the primary bow (from inside out) are always violet, blue, green, yellow, orange, and red, depending on how they blend one into the other. This is caused by the refraction of light through water molecules. Another key feature is the "rainbow angle", or placement of the sun (in this case the radiant moon), relative to both the observer and the water in the atmosphere. Specifically, the axis of two lines, one formed by the sun's rays shining down through you, and the second formed from the eye to the rainbow itself, is always forty-two degrees.

However, this vision went beyond the scientifically explainable, and entered the realm of the spiritual. It touched my core, and Zajonc's words rang true: I imagined this light, myself, and the world around me as a richer and deeper place. Rather than merely having a mechanical understanding of what I saw, I dwelled lovingly in this new phenomenon. The essence of this light was not just a physical thing, an idol, but a spiritual reality.

It wasn't until several weeks later, as I retold this story to friends, that it became clear the spiritual depth of my experience. This wonderful, magical silver light juxtaposed against the onyx-like sky, truly was a moment with our Creator. I realized then, as a shiver resonated through my entire body, that I witnessed the portal for the soul's retreat to heaven. Nature's most cherished gift, the gateway to immortality, was welcoming all those innocent passengers and crew from Flight 111 to their final resting place.

THE CANADIAN NOSTRADAMUS

John Robert Colombo

The Canadian Nostradamus?

Herein lies the story ...

But before I begin, some information is necessary. There are two questions that have to be answered here. The first question has a straightforward answer. The second question is not that easily answered.

Here is the first question: *Did Nostradamus predict the tragedy of September 11, 2001?*

In other words, was Michel de Nostre Dame (1503–1566), the French physician and prophet known today as Nostradamus, able to foresee and describe in his usual veiled terms the crash of hijacked jetliners into the twin towers of the World Trade Center in New York City, into the Pentagon in Washington, D.C., and into the rural field in Pennsylvania?

The answer to that question is simplicity itself: No, even the most persistent proponent of the works of the sixteenth-century prophet would be at a loss to point to even a single quatrain in the French text of his *Prophecies* (1555) or in the numerous English translations and commentaries that predicts (or even seems to predict) the terrorists' attack.

I paged through a popular *en face* edition — Charles A. Ward's *Oracles of Nostradamus* (New York: Modern Library, 1940) — and even by stretching the matter could find nothing that merited consideration. Nor is there any reference that could conceivably shed light on the tragedy in John Hogue's exhaustive tome *Nostradamus: The Complete Prophecies* (Shaftesbury, Dorset: Element, 1997).

So much for the first question. Nostradamus did not predict 9/11.

Here is the second question: *Did a Canadian acting in the guise of Nostradamus predict the tragedy?*

As I suggested, the answer here is somewhat less than satisfactory. It seems — I repeat, it seems — that an Ontario student did make a prediction that was pressed into service by promoters of the writings of Nostradamus and North American news services.

Here is what happened.

The day following the terrorist attacks on the World Trade Center in New York City on September 11, 2001, e-mails and wire services carried the following quatrain, which was attributed to the sixteenth-century French seer Nostradamus:

> In the City of God there will be a great thunder,
> Two brothers torn apart by Chaos,
> While the fortress endures, the great leader will succumb,
> The third big war will begin when the big city is burning.
> — Nostradamus, 1654

The year is obviously wrong. Nostradamus could not have composed the quatrain in 1654; he died in 1566. "City of God" is a far-fetched description of Manhattan, even for Nostradamus. Yet the reference to "the big city" burning is arresting, as is the account of the destruction of the twin towers ("two brothers") that precipitates a world war ("the third big war"). They seem tailor-made for the occasion.

Were they tailor-made? Composed after the events had occurred?

Once the quatrain was published in newspapers around the world, the Internet book service Amazon.com reported that sales of Nostradamus's books had soared. But subsequent news stories dismissed the verse as a hoax. For instance, Daniel Swift, writing in "Letter from New York," *Times Literary Supplement*, October 5, 2001, noted: "These lines seem nearly to predict the destruction of the World Trade Center, and were discussed and quoted on the news; but they turned out to be a hoax, not written by Nostradamus at all, but concocted by a student in Ontario four years ago in order to debunk Nostradamus."

News stories noted that the lines were actually composed by Neil Marshall, a student at Brock University, St. Catharines, Ontario. In

1997, when he was a high-school student, he was inspired to write them for a website that meant to demonstrate how the writings of the seer could be twisted. Marshall claimed authorship of the first three lines; he suggested that the last line was added by someone else to make the warning sound even more prescient.

It has been said that Marshall based his own lines on the following English translation by an unknown hand of Nostradamus's quatrain (Century 6, Quatrain 97):

> Five and forty steps the sky will burn
> Fire approaching the large new city
> Instantly a great thin flame will leap
> When someone will want to test the Normans.

Ward's edition translates the original French in this fashion: "At 45 degrees [Lyon] the heaven shall burn, the fire shall come near to the great new city, instantly a great scattered flame shall leap forth when one shall see the Normans make an attempt."

Henry C. Roberts in *The Complete Prophecies of Nostradamus* (New York: Nostradamus, Inc., 1947; 17th printing, 1970) offers this translation of the quatrain:

> The heaven shall burn at five and forty degrees,
> the fire shall come near the great new city,
> In an instant a great flame dispersed shall burst out,
> When they shall make a trial of the Normans.

Was Neil Marshall as inspired as the commentators?

This much was reported by wire services and e-mail suppliers. I undertook a bit of research myself. I was unable to locate the website in question. I was unable to locate the Brock student, or former student, Neil Marshall.

No more successful than I was Eric McMillan, chairman of the Ontario Skeptics Society for Critical Inquiry, who informed me on October 19, 2001, that a brief search to track Marshall down was unsuccessful.

Was the quatrain composed by an unidentified journalist who then attributed it to a high school student to whom he gave the name Neil Marshall?

Why has the former high school student not stepped forward?

It seems that Neil Marshall, when he writes in the prophetic manner of Nostradamus, is himself as mysterious as the French prophet!

Of mysteries there are no ends!

So Neil Marshall, if he exists, is the Canadian Nostradamus.

I might add that as Canadians we are generally described as modest, unassuming people who hide our talents under bushel baskets. But modesty is not a virtue identified with prophecy. Who ever heard of a modest Nostradamus?

THE ART OF COLD READING

The Amazing Randi is the stage name of James Randi, illusionist, escape artist, and debunker of claims of the paranormal. Randi was born in Toronto and raised in Montreal. He now lives in Florida, but his travels take him to the capitals of the world, where he performs and lectures and captivates audiences.

At a young age he honed his skills as a mentalist at Toronto's Canadian National Exhibition, and in his youth he worked as a writer for Montreal's tabloid press and as a broadcaster for the city's English-language radio stations. After moving to New Jersey and then to Florida, he took a leaf from Houdini's book of magic tricks and trained as an escape artist. Taking a second leaf from Houdini's book, he became a critic of those mediums and trance channellers who prey on the public's credulity.

"The Art of Cold Reading" is a lively memoir, but it is also his incisive criticism of how psychic readings are accomplished. A "cold reading" is one given by a self-styled psychic who has to improvise — make vague statements to the subject, ask leading questions, construct scenarios based on clues, etc. A "hot reading" is one given by the operator who has at his or her disposal advance information about the subject.

This article originally appeared on the website of the James Randi Educational Foundation on October 28, 2001.

The Art of Cold Reading

James Randi

The currently popular "psychics" like Sylvia Browne, James Van Praagh, and John Edward, who are getting so much TV space on

Montel Williams, Larry King, and other shows, employ a technique known as "cold reading."

They tell the subjects nothing, but make guesses, put out suggestions, and ask questions. This is a very deceptive art, and the unwary observer may come away believing that unknown data was developed by some wondrous means. Not so.

Examples: "I get an older man here" is a question, a suggestion, and a guess by the "reader," who expects some reaction from the subject, and usually gets it. That reaction may just be a nod, the actual name of a person, or an identification (brother, husband, grandfather), but it is supplied *by the subject*, not by the reader. "They're saying, 'Bob' or 'Robert.' Do you recognize this person?" is another question, suggestion, and guess. If there's a Bob or Robert, the subject will amplify the identification. But if there's no Bob or Robert immediately recognized, the reader passes right on, after commenting that Bob is there alright, but not recognized right now. If any Bob is remembered later, that is incorporated into the spiel.

You should observe and listen to a video of a reading. In one such by Van Praagh, prepared by the *48 Hours* TV program, a reading that lasted 60 minutes, we found only *two* actual statements made, and 260 questions asked. Both actual statements — guesses — were wrong. Van Praagh was looking for the name of the woman's deceased husband, and he came up with it by asking, "Do you know anyone named Jack?" The woman answered, "Yes! Jack, my husband!" But Van Praagh didn't identify "Jack" at all. He asked her if *she* would identify him. By that time, Van Praagh had already tried on her 26 other men's names — all wrong. But, the woman — the subject — forgot about those failures, because they were not important to her. "Jack" was important. The readers have a way of leading the subject to believe that they knew something they didn't.

Example: Reader: "Did your husband linger on in the hospital, or did he pass quickly?"

Subject: "Oh, he died almost immediately!"

Reader: "Yes, because he's saying to me, 'I didn't suffer. I was spared any pain.'"

It's strange that the reader (Van Praagh, in this example) had to ask that question…

And remember, these readers often go out and interview the audience members when they're in line waiting to get into the studio or auditorium.

That technique was employed by the very successful reader Doris Stokes. She would feed back any data she got as if she were refreshing her memory of what had been told her. "Are you the lady who has a passed-on sister, dearie?" would of course receive assent from the victim, and ahhhs from the audience.

Also, a person who approaches the reader before the TV show or auditorium meeting and says she has a question about her deceased grandmother, can then later be selected out of the audience when they're on-camera or during the live encounter, and can then be asked, "Is your question about your grandmother?" and that appears — to everyone else — like a bang-on "hit."

Or, and this is very subtle indeed, people in the studio or auditorium audience — usually seated up front for best visibility — are sometimes those who have already been to the "psychic" for a private reading, and have then been asked to show up later to occupy reserved seats at the public in-person gathering "to develop more information" using the "collective power of the assembled audience." The reader then repeats previously gleaned data, and that appears miraculous both to the audience in the studio and at home, watching, or elsewhere in the auditorium audience.

We tested Sylvia Browne in 1989, on live TV, and she failed miserably. On that occasion, she was not allowed to speak to anyone in advance, or to be asked or told anything in advance. The audience was told to only answer "yes" or "no" when asked a *direct* question, and Sylvia bombed out big-time. She blamed it all on bad vibrations.... Van Praagh and Edward have not responded to our offer to test them — for the million-dollar prize, even.

So, you see, it's your perception of what's actually being done, rather that the reality of the procedure, and your ignorance of other subtle clues and methods, that misleads you in your observations of these "psychics."

I'll give you one example of something I did when I was performing as a mentalist in Toronto, my home town, at the age of eighteen. (I hasten to add here that I would *always* thoroughly disclaim any genuine powers, before and after my show.) They had a huge auditorium filled with reserved seats, just about every one of them occupied by eager subjects. It was some sort of a charity affair, and seats were expensive.

After I got rolling with the various moving objects and blindfolded duplication-of-handwriting stunts (spoon-bending was not yet a popular miracle!), I stopped abruptly and pointed to a lady in the third-row aisle seat. "I'm led to say to you that I get a middle name of 'Rose' for you, madame!" I cried. Her gasp verified that I was right. "And that name is more than significant to you." She leaned forward. "I see a clock, a very old clock, and on the dial three pink roses?" She started to speak, and I silenced her by raising my hand. "But this is a strange clock. It can't tell the time!" By now, the poor woman was about to pass out in excitement. "Why is it useless? I see two arrows, or darts! They're metal, and they're broken! Ah! I see! These are the hands of that clock, and they've come off the clock face, and are lying together behind the glass cover of the clock dial! Is that right?" The woman was standing, mouth open, nodding vigorously. She was awe-struck, and the applause was vigorous indeed.

How was it done? A lucky guess? No. Planning.

T.K. Lawson, my buddy, had been working with that charity. He was the one who got me the gig (a contracted appearance). And he also went through several neighborhoods selling tickets to likely donors. He had sold tickets CC-20 and CC-22 to this lady, and she'd invited him into her living-room while she made out a check to pay for the tickets. He observed that the "rose" theme was everywhere, and an embroidered "sampler" was framed by the door, with the woman's full name on it. That clock was by the fireplace. T.K. noted these facts and reported them to me.

I must tell you that together we intercepted that dear lady as she left after the show and explained to her how I'd been "psychic." She was highly entertained with the explanation and grateful for our caring to tell her.

I somehow don't think that Browne, Edward, and Van Praagh would trouble to do such a thing. But, after all, they say they're *really* "speaking with the dead." I'm amazed at how much death affects people who undergo the process. It makes them really stupid and forgetful. Whenever I've asked any psychics — or spiritualists — to contact my paternal grandmother, it seems she doesn't remember such basics as the name of her husband, or the name of her church — both important elements in her life while she was "here." Now that she's "there," her rather prodigious intellect has left her quite completely.

THE LADY WITH THE LAMP

A few days before Christmas 2001, I received an unusual Christmas gift. It took the form of a letter with an enclosure sent to me by William Thornton-Trump, a resident of Surrey, British Columbia.

The correspondent was a gentleman unknown to me, but he may well have been familiar with my work as a collector of accounts of supernatural and paranormal experiences. The letter he sent was dated December 15, 2001, and in it he explained that he was writing to me on behalf of his brother, Sandy. Here is what he wrote:

> I enclose a story by my brother, Alexander Thornton-Trump. A friend suggested that you might find this story interesting.
>
> As my brother has little remaining eyesight, I have edited and formatted the story, but it is his story.
>
> I hope that you might find it to be of interest and perhaps suitable for publication. In any case, please let me know. You can contact me either at the above address or at the e-mail address at the end of this letter.

Needless to say I read the enclosed story and marvelled at the experience and the telling. I replied by e-mail requesting a few particulars. Mr. Thornton-Thump replied by e-mail on December 28, 2001:

> Thank you for your kind remarks about my brother's story.
>
> He and I have been working on this together, but since he lives in Winnipeg and I am near Vancouver, there is a certain time lag. I can tell you that he is

delighted, though, to know that it will be published. In a recent e-mail he said:

> I think it is wonderful that the little Ukrainian-Canadian town of Senkiw (now comprising one Ukranian Orthodox Church with onion dome and seating for at least a dozen people), one small community hall with Senkiw painted on a board in an arc over the door, and two outhouses, shall finally have one of its catastrophes noticed.

You asked:

> "In the meantime, could you send me some particulars about your brother, such as his age at the time of the occurrence, the place where it occurred, and any other relevant details."

My brother, Alexander Thornton-Trump, has taught Engineering at the University of Manitoba for many years. Since he mentions in the narrative that the incident took place in 1980, and since he is now 61, he would have been around 40 at the time.

I had never heard of Senkiw before reading his story (and the above description explains why!) but I assume that it is near Winnipeg, since I know that my brother has some land around there.

In any case, he would be able to answer any specific questions much better than I. You can contact him directly by e-mail.

While his actual name is Alexander, he is known to everybody as Sandy.

Finally, as you requested, I am attaching the story to this e-mail in Word Document format.

So I am in the debt of the two Thornton-Trumps for the chance to read this account and for the opportunity to share "The Lady with the Lamp" with my readers. I like it because it is a rattling good story, and a true one at that. I find it to be convincing because of its origin, and because it fits to a T the pattern of so many rural hauntings.

It was a wonderful Christmas gift!

N.B. It was followed by a New Year's gift, which arrived on December 31, 2001. The gift took the form of another e-mail from Sandy's brother:

Dear Mr. Colombo,

Today I received an e-mail from my brother Sandy containing the information that I copy below. I thought you might like to see it:

I met the Lady with the Lamp when I was 39, the year after I had purchased the five acres on which the first school house for the town of Senkiw had been built. The town had been founded by a group of Ukrainian immigrants who migrated to Canada in 1911. The homestead land was very poor since it was not in the Red River Valley, but up on a sandy bench left behind when Lake Agassiz drained. The land had only a few inches of top soil and had been covered in Manitoba bush, a combination of small poplar trees, bush oak and a variety of wild plum, saskatoon and other low bushes. Senkiw is located to the east of the Red River approximately seventy kilometers south of Winnipeg.

While the town of Senkiw no longer exists as a town, the church and the town hall are still in use for special events of the people who still form, in their own minds, the spirit of Senkiw. The school house was moved in the 1920s to a location near the town hall, then abandoned sometime in the late '40s.

The language of the community is still substantially Ukrainian, but the newest generation seems to be losing that. The Lady with the Lamp spoke to me in Ukrainian, was rather well-dressed considering the lack of wealth of the community, and wearing what was possibly a beaver coat. Beavers are always damming the creek and flooding my 160 acres of woods. In the story I did not do justice to her panic and near hysteria.

As my brother has told you, I teach Engineering at the University of Manitoba and continue to do so. At the time of the meeting of the Lady, we were building a garage on the property next to the old wagon track that connected Senkiw to the small town of Rosa. We keep the trail open out of a sense of historical duty, as do the neighbours on their portion. Across the township road there is a Ukrainian house of the traditional mud wattle and white plaster construction, built in 1917, and Mr. Andrushko helped us build our garage. He was the last of that family line to live in the house.

Will Trump
Surrey, B.C.
Canada

The Lady with the Lamp

Alexander (Sandy) Thornton-Trump

We had a cloth-top camper trailer back in 1980 and had gone out to the farm to clear the young poplar shoots from the area where I wished to build a garage in which to keep the machinery I was accumulating for my experiments in silvaculture.

It was mid-October, a beautiful Indian summer day of soft winds, warm sun, blue skies, and green grass. The air smelled sweet with the ancient grasses of the prairie that still grow in my bit of wild woods and glades. That evening we made dinner on the campfire and listened to the whippoorwill calling as dusk turned to dark. Under a black clear sky, the stars shining in their millions from the Milky Way, we put the kids to bed, and they slept deeply as we talked a bit, then turned in ourselves.

The camper was parked on a small, flat-topped mound that had once served as the base for a schoolmaster's house. We had purchased the five-acre block that was the old Senkiw school site. The school on this site had been built in 1912, then moved to a new location about a mile away around 1918. So, in this historical setting we went to bed and I zipped up the canvas flap and we went to sleep.

The tapping on the metal was insistent. I awoke slowly, aware of the wind whistling around the camper and the continued tapping. I got up and unzipped the tent flap and was startled by a white face, large dark eyes, and beautiful dark hair. The young woman carried a hurricane lantern of unusual construction, and she was dressed in a heavy coat, scarf, and fur hat. She was obviously very upset and frantically asking or pleading with me for something. I put on my heavy, fleece-lined coat, my heavy boots, and climbed out of the camper to follow her.

The transformation of the surroundings was startling. Heavy snow was swirling down, an accumulation of about ten inches beginning to drift heavily in the exposed areas. We set off on the Rosa to Senkiw trail that ran through my woods, crossed a field, and entered another wooded area.

Here I found a horse with a two-wheeled carriage that was stuck, the wheels off the road in a drift of snow. The woman mounted the carriage and encouraged the horse to try again. I put my back against a wheel, grasped the rough spoke of the large wheel, and heaved, and the carriage moved.

I watched the light retreat with the carriage, but the light went from one side of the trail to the other, as if the woman were hunting for something. She called out something in a Slavic language, a little like the Russian which I had heard in my youth. I trudged back to the camper and climbed in, cleaning off my boots and shaking the snow off my coat, then went back to bed.

In the morning I woke up to silence and was pleased the wind had stopped, but knew I would have trouble getting the car out and home in all the snow. I unzipped the flap and was stunned. There was no snow. The grass was green and the sun was filtering through the bare branches of the poplars from a perfect blue sky. A heavy dew sparkled on the field.

But the dream was such a reality!

George, a neighbour, invited us over for lunch with some of the local farmers, all of Ukrainian ancestry. At one point Bill Smook said, "It was just like this the day before the great storm. The lady with the lamp will be out looking for her son."

"What do you mean?" I asked.

"Back in 1912 it started to snow heavily at noon in mid-October. The schoolmaster sent all the children home so they could get there safely before the storm got really bad and the snow plugged the road. Late that day the mother of one of the small boys showed up at the schoolmaster's house and asked for her son, but he had left with the other children. She left the schoolmaster, saying she would keep looking and asked him to get help. The weather turned cold right after the snow, and neither she nor the boy was ever seen again. But sometimes, at this time of year, people claim they see her walking up the old road with her lamp, looking for her son. She is the local ghost."

"I know," I said. "I met her last night." And in the shocked silence around the table, I told them my story and watched the colour drain from their faces.

Well, I own much of that old trail today, and in certain places I could swear I feel the fear and panic of that woman. I feel her grief and her pain and her love.

GHOST STORIES

Here is a cheery letter about a serious motorcycle accident that could have claimed the lives of the correspondent Rodney Coreau and his brother Chris. Rodney was prompted to write to me while reading a copy of my book *Ghost Stories of Canada*. He wonders about the Sandy Hill district. A mystery or two about the district in Ottawa where said-to-be-haunted Laurier House is located appear *Mysteries of Ontario*.

Rodney closes his e-mail with lines of verse from Tolkein's *Lord of the Rings*. I will reproduce a couplet here rather than at the end, as they set the tone for what will follow.

> The Road goes ever on and on
> Down from the door where it began.

Ghost Stories

Rodney Coreau

From: rodney coreau
To: jrc@inforamp.net
Subject: Ghost Stories of Canada
Date: Saturday, August 03, 2002 11:54 PM

Hello Mr. Colombo:

It's just after 11:00 P.M. here in Ottawa and I was in the middle of your book and just wanted to take this time to express my appreciation ... plus I was getting a little creeped out and needed a break!

I was in the middle of the accounts of the Mackenzie residence in Toronto, when the sudden blare siren from the streets below my balcony made me jump. Well, I would use the term "scared the hell out of me." Sometimes you never know how far into something you are, until you're yanked back!

I've been an avid lover of ghost stories from a very young age and I would love to experience one, even though I am certain a small measure of bladder control would be lost.

I'm not all the way through it yet, but I haven't seen any mention of Ottawa's Sandy Hill district. A very old beautiful neighborhood with a bit of a dark side in its own right. I had the opportunity of taking a haunted walk through there one night, a tour that left from The Famous ... or infamous ... Nicholas Street Hostel and toured such sites as Mackenzie King's old residence where he had many conversations with his late mother. The Hostel, you probably know, is haunted, being an old jail and the site of Canada's last public hanging. But perhaps these stories are a little more well known. I think the Hostel might have been done to death, if you'll pardon the pun.

Myself, the only experience of note I have had I would really put in the category of Angel rather than Ghost, as it was unseen. And while it might not be historically significant, being relative of course to how well known I end up being after my death, it's an encounter I can't easily explain.

My older brother, Chris, and I were out on a tour on a four wheeler in the fields around our home, just outside Arnprior, Ontario. It was a nice, partly cloudy, summer day. It was just the two of us because both our parents worked and it was summer vacation.

I was driving and Chris was on the back. We came to a short, but very steep incline, that had to be about five feet in height. Definitely more than forty-five degrees, and it scared me so I stopped dead just before it.

My brother was egging me on. "What are you waiting for? Go for it!" And rather than look like a wimp in front of my brother, a concern that usually takes precedence over good sense in a young man's mind, I put it in gear and floored it. At the top of it was a big smooth rock. Our front tire hit it, which sent the bike onto its back tires and my brother and I off onto the ground, I guess a good six or seven foot drop because we were at the top of the hill on the bike at the time.

Chris landed first and then myself on top of him, with nothing to see but the very heavy bike looming over me on its back tires and the engine still roaring, not having died down yet since my hand fell from the throttle. I remember thinking, "I'm dead, this is it, this thing is going to crush us." It seemed to me the upward momentum of the bike, bucking us off like a horse, should have kept the front end continuing in an arc and following us to the ground and crushing us like I had been thinking. But it just sort of hanged there for a second on its two back wheels and then went to its side on top of the incline. Like something grabbed it and stopped it. Or maybe the laws of physics at the time favoured such an unlikely move. Or maybe that's how angels work in the first place. Whatever force is responsible, I thought it was nice of them. Getting crushed by an eight-hundred-plus-pound bike would have ruined my day.

I shall definitely be buying another one of your books though! If you wrote about the Sandy Hill region in Ottawa I'd love to know which book.

Take care, keep your spirits up.

Rodney

THE GHOST IN THE HEALTH CLUB

The following account comes from the October 2000 issue of the monthly newsletter of the Toronto Ghosts and Hauntings Research Society.

The newsletter is an e-mail publication. The TGHRS is headed by a most personable and resourceful computer specialist named Matthew Didier. The society may be reached through its website: *www.torontoghosts.org.*

It is TGHRS's policy to withhold names of informants and witnesses. There are some good reasons to respect the identity of the men and women who share accounts of their weird experiences. At the same time there are good reasons to eschew the policy of anonymity. Some day I might explore the pros and cons.

In my books I generally publish names and addresses as applicable. But in the past I have honoured the occasional request for anonymity, based on the circumstances, usually asking the witness to choose a pseudonym, as I am not much impressed with "Anon." as a contributor! In the meantime, I have no problem publishing "The Ghost in the Health Club" as by "Anonymous" because the identity of the experiencer is known to Matthew Didier and I trust him that the account is on the up-and-up. (The Editor's note that appears in the second e-mailed letter is Matthew's, not mine!)

It certainly reads well!

The Ghost in the Health Club

Health Club Member

Hi Matthew …

I admit that I'm a little ... okay, a LOT plump. I've recently been working out and looking into local gyms to hopefully start the fight against my spare tire. (I often joke that some men have abs like a six pack, I have a keg!)

I went to a rather famous downtown gym and was chatting it up with one of the managers of it and on my second visit, he remarked that he had seen me on a local Toronto television show and as such, wanted to discuss his own "ghost story" with me. I listened to him and we were even joined by another employee who also had experiences in the gym. After a bit, I asked if I could use it. Sadly, the club owners do NOT want the story out and about and after a bit of good old-fashioned horse trading, he agreed to send me the story via e-mail to use here AS LONG AS I didn't mention his name, the name of the gym or it's location. Not great for our website but good for here ... It's an interesting story.

Needless to say, it's been edited rather heavily.

Hi Matthew ...

I started working at the gym over seven years ago and have done almost every job you can do here. We've trained athletes of all types and some have gone on to become great champions of their chosen sports and some were already established and have come in to hone their skills. It's a great job.

My second week there, I was asked to help closing the gym (we close VERY late at night), and I started collecting loose equipment and generally tidying up.

On my way out of one of the rooms, I switched off the lights. Seconds later, as I was just closing the door, the lights went back on by themselves. I reached in and shut them off again, started closing the door and CLICK! They went on again.

I figured that the switch was just sticking or something so I went back in the room and switched the light off hard and held it down for a while. I removed my hand and the lights stayed off and after a few minutes, I felt that the lights were off for good.

I walked to the door and as it was swinging shut, CLICK! The lights went on again!

Needless to say, I didn't think it was anything paranormal and yelled out "Shoot!" [Editor's note: This was not what the author shouted but it is a PG newsletter.]

The person helping me close up came over and said, "What's wrong?"

I explained to him the problems I was having with the lights. He went ... "Oh! That's just George. We'll have to ask him if we can turn out the lights. GEORGE! WE'RE CLOSING UP NOW AND HAVE TO TURN OUT THE LIGHTS, SORRY!"

He walked into the room and turned off the lights with no problem. He came back to me at the door and closed the door and the lights stayed off this time.

I didn't believe it. I had to know who or what George was. He told me that many years before, a boxer named George was training when all of a sudden, he just fell over dead after a sparring round in the gym. There was no reason for this, as George was a healthy man. This guy said he thinks he heard George had a stroke of sorts but wasn't sure. He said that since then, George haunts the gym and occasionally causes problems.

I didn't believe this ... well, not really. I just sort of accepted the story and we left the gym for a beer together where he shared more stories about George. George played with lights, took equipment out of lockers, opened and closed doors and occasionally was seen (maybe) in the showers.

The staff all accepted George as he never did anything mean or really harmful.

The story was a good one and after that, whenever anything went wrong, everyone would just say, "Oh, it's just George!"

About a year later, I was working very late alone and had to lock up myself. I had earlier lost my watch in the locker rooms and wasted a lot of time looking for it and so had to work late to catch up on some paperwork.

I got up from my desk in the office and (as was everyone's custom who worked there) I said in a loud voice, "Thanks George. I'm going home now and have to lock up! I'll see you tomorrow!"

With that, I did the rounds, turned off the lights and was leaving through the main doors when I heard something make a metallic sounding "thunk" noise in the middle of our ring.

I went over to investigate and there, in the middle of the ring, was my watch.

All afternoon, people had been sparring and using the ring and no one had noticed my watch? What could I do? I was happy so I said, "Thanks, George!" and locked up and went home.

Customers and staff have seen doors open and close by themselves, and staff members are very fond of our ghost. George is as much a fixture in the gym as any piece of equipment.

There are many more stories of George's antics. One time, he turned on every light in the place at three in the morning, which led the local police to come and investigate. The owner had to come in and say, "Don't worry, it's nothing," but didn't tell them about George.

Once, in the middle of a busy Saturday afternoon, George turned out all the lights in the place. All the electronic equipment was on but all the lights went out! I remember that you [Matthew] mentioned that was weird because we use a mix of fluorescent and incandescent light bulbs. That was the only time George ever scared me. Not only did the lights all go out but the temperature in the gym dropped to freezing! After a few seconds, it all came back to normal. I wonder what bothered George that day?

Like I said, George has even been seen. I can't tell you who, but once we stayed open very late for a famous athlete to work out alone. He wanted privacy and must have paid the owner a ton of money. I got stuck waiting for him to finish to lock up.

After he finished, he went to the showers and in a few minutes, I heard him yell, "Hey!"

I thought he'd run out of hot water or something but that wasn't it. He came out and was very shaken. He said he'd seen man in boxing gear sitting just outside the showers. He yelled because he was upset to see someone else in the gym besides himself and me and was going to yell at the man for being there.

Just as he was going to get out of the shower to grab the man, he vanished.

I told him all about George and he seemed to be very upset. What's cool is that after I told him about George, he and I sat down and he told me all about a ghost in a house he lived at in Georgia when he was playing for another team. He told me that he likes looking for ghosts but didn't like running into one at a gym, especially while he was showering!

Well, that's my story. Please make sure you keep my name and the gym's name out of it, as the owner is not as happy with George as we are. He's even threatened an exorcism!

[Editor's note: An exorcism at a gym ... HAHAHAHAHA!]

This gym is VERY busy in the early evenings and I find it weird that the three staff I've spoken to (at different times) all know and seem to love George!

George seems very happy in his gym and I guess he may really like the concept of spending eternity working out and sparring at his leisure with only those annoying "live" people cramping his workout!

I hope that the only exorcise that George gets is his rope jumping. (Unless, of course, one day he makes it clear that he wants to leave!)

THE DREAM VISIT

I am indebted to Charlotte Fielden Morris for sending me this vivid account of a "dream visit" on January 28, 2003. It was prepared by her friend, the actress Helen Hughes, whose list of stage and screen credits is wide, including leads in plays by Michel Tremblay and John Murrell as well as roles in such feature films as *Outrageous* (1977), *The Incubus* (1982), *The Amityville Curse* (1990), *The Rapture* (1993), *Night of the Twisters* (1996), *Harlan Country War* (2000), etc.

In her account Hughes records, in both prose and poetry, what is known in parapsychology as a crisis apparition — the appearance at the point of death of the spirit of the deceased. It is a form of bilocation in extremis. In this instance it takes place during deep sleep, though sometimes it is recorded as happening during a daytime reverie or at the points of entering or leaving the state of sleep. What to make of it? The experience is subjective, circumstantial, and highly personal. It is invariably surprising. It mostly enriches upon reflection. It usually marks the moment of closure, of coming to terms with mortality ... and perhaps immortality.

The Dream Visit

Helen Hughes

Before I describe the unusual event that I dreamt about, I should explain that when it occurred in 1995, I was happily married and living in Toronto. I had three grown children by two previous marriages. The second marriage was to A., who left me after twenty-three years to "try to regain his youth" with a very young woman. The marriage had ended in divorce. But we had remained on fairly friendly terms; after all, we had been friends since high school.

The dream visit occurred fifteen years after the divorce. I had spent several weeks shooting a film in Montreal. That evening I was looking forward to going to bed early, to having a good sleep, and then breakfast in the hotel, a day of leisure, and a late-afternoon pick-up call that would take me to the set. I was fighting a cold that had infiltrated the cast and I was asleep by 11:00 p.m.

I was travelling on a rapidly moving train. I was sitting on the lap of a young beach-bum type of guy who was trying to coax me into staying on the train and then going kayaking with him. I kept refusing, telling him I had to get off at my stop. As I looked forward in the train, I saw A., my ex-husband, seated by himself, watching me reproachfully. He was sitting near the front of the carriage on the opposite side of the aisle.

I unwound myself from the young man's lap and walked up the aisle. As I came to A.'s seat, he looked at me sadly, and said, "Aren't you going to kiss me goodbye?"

I leaned over to kiss him, but his face was soft and grey and his lips had no resisting pressure. It was like kissing a balloon that had mostly deflated. I continued to make my way to the front of the carriage and exited when the train stopped.

When I awoke from the dream, I was drenched in sweat and felt awful. Some time later, at about six o'clock in the morning, my youngest son phoned me to tell me that A. had died during the night.

Through all the years I had known A., I had never once dreamt of him. Normally I cannot remember dreams, but eight years later, this one is still vivid in my memory.

All through A.'s life, from high-school years through university to a distinguished teaching career, he was relentlessly intellectual. He made no secret that he was envious of my social skills and my artistic abilities in theatre, music, and painting.

A week after the shoot in Montreal was over, I was still shaking from the dream visit. I wrote the following poem about the dream visit. It is dated November 17, 1995:

On a rushing train,
In my deepest sleep he found me.
Followed me with accusing eyes,
His greying face sticky with tears.
"I am alone, I am cold," he said.
"Why are you so happy?
Why do you laugh?
Why the jasmine-scent in your hair?
Why are you warm?
Why this voice of bells?
I am on this side, and you are still there.
Don't go," he cried.
But I left him on the relentless train,
The train he built on his own tracks
Going to his own station.

INSTANCES OF PRESCIENCE

"You must have a wonderful life," the voice at the other end of the line said.

"What do you mean?" I asked.

"You meet such interesting people and they tell you such strange experiences about their encounters with ghosts. And then you can publish them!"

"You're right," I said. "But I don't always meet these interesting people. Sometimes I do, but more often than not the communication is by phone, letter, or e-mail. But the initial excitement of hearing or reading their stories is followed by the hard work of keyboarding the accounts, readying them for publication in book form, finding a publisher to issue that book, and then waiting the year or so for that book to appear. It's an avocation, not a vocation. And it's more pleasurable than it is profitable!"

But, in a way, it *is* a wonderful life!

A case in point is Helen Hughes. I have seen her on the stage and on the screen, and we reside in the same city, and in the same section of Toronto, but still ahead of me lies the pleasure of meeting her in person.

She is a friend of a friend, and it was through that friend, Charlotte Fielden, that I have been corresponding with Ms. Hughes, who initially sent me her account of "The Dream Visit," followed by these accounts of her four odd experiences. I have titled these "Instances of Prescience." They were written on February 16, 2003.

I wonder what odd and unusual experiences await Ms. Hughes in the years that lie ahead …

Instances of Prescience

Helen Hughes

1.

Around nine-thirty one snowy winter morning, I was driving my little VW from my home in the country outside Durham, N.H., to a rehearsal at a theatre in Portsmouth. I had driven the route many times — sometimes twice daily — for six years. I passed through the town of Durham to the point where the road forked. Straight ahead went to Portsmouth, and left to Dover.

After five or ten minutes, I became aware — woke up? — to find myself in Dover. Cursing my stupidity, and knowing I'd be late for rehearsal, I angrily wheeled the car around in the nearest ploughed-out driveway and headed back to the fork.

I got on the Portsmouth road, and had not gone far when I was met by flashing lights, police cars, ambulances, and a horrific, three-car accident. That was just where I would have been had I not made a "mistake."

I arrived at the rehearsal for *Long Day's Journey into Night* — late, and shaking in my boots, still trying to understand what had happened.

2.

Once I was awakened, scared to death, by a picture in my head.

A large plane crossed the frame from right to left. As it neared the centre, there was a brilliant blue flash from its tail, and it dived to earth.

I felt uneasy because it was so vivid and had to reason with myself to get back to sleep.

"It's only a dream," I thought. "Even if I've had prescience, I don't know the destination or airline or anything."

The next day, the picture, just as I saw it, was on the front page of the newspaper.

3.

In 1969, my daughter Paula was working as a model in New York, London, and Paris. She had sent me copies of all her "spreads" and pictures from *Vogue*, *Harper's*, *Mademoiselle*, *Elle*, etc., and I had stored them in a big bundle in a bottom drawer.

One morning, for no reason at all, I made a cup of tea and spread them all out on the breakfast counter. As I looked at them again, the phone rang.

It was Paula. She seemed hesitant, so I asked her why she had called. "I don't know," she said, "I was just sitting here in my hotel room, having a cup of tea, and felt I should call you."

As we talked, she gradually let me know she was unhappy with the sterility of life as a model, and was going out with a man whom she didn't really trust. I reassured her of my faith in her ability and strength, and told her I'd just been looking at her work.

She doesn't call me often, but while I was writing this account in 2003, the phone rang. It was Paula, calling from Paris, for no particular reason.

4.

One morning, I was doing yoga exercises, finishing with a headstand. I don't know how long I'd been on my head, when the phone rang. It was someone I had not ever expected to hear from — a man who had been an actor in the theatre where I worked. After his play closed, he had gone back to New York to look for work, and was, instead, waiting on tables.

He had no reason for calling me. "I just felt I had to," he said.

Was it because he was the person who introduced me to yoga and taught me to stand on my head? He had never called me before, and my only contact with him had been the free daily yoga lessons he gave us, and of course, the times we were on stage together. But I guess we had bonded in some subtle way.

ROY'S STORY

The still point around which this story revolves is the person of Betty Stewart.

Betty was a remarkable woman. People who met her never forgot her, nor did she ever forget them. She was both personable and formidable. She felt she was in contact with extraterrestrial intelligences and that they were sharing with her secrets of vital interest.

She was once the subject an hour-long episode of CBC-TV's *Man Alive*. That was at the time when the television series was hosted and largely scripted by the affable and genial Roy Bonisteel. The episode dealt with the subject of alien encounters, and Betty left no one in doubt that she was in command of her senses and (just possibly) in contact with alien intelligences. The program generated a lot of viewer response.

I met her a few years later and the first thing I did was convince her that she should write out an account of her experiences with the aliens, the Retriculan greys, so described by Budd Hopkins, whom she knew personally. Goaded on by a mutual friend, Joyce Halfin, Betty did so. The stylish memoir appears in my collection *UFOs over Canada*.

A few years later I also convinced Betty that she should appear with me on the thirty-minute daily television program hosted by the veteran broadcaster Bob McLean. His show was then being produced at a television station in Kitchener. Betty told her story to Bob and stole the show. People remembered seeing her on the show, not me. That was all right with me because I felt she really enjoyed the spotlight, had something to say, and really connected with people ... and possibly with aliens, too!

That show was seen by Anita Welsh, the next contributor to this collection. I knew nothing about this fact until about five years later, when Willa McLean, Bob's charming wife and program organizer, phoned me about another television appearance. During the conversation she reminded me of "the Betty Stewart" program and the buzz that it had occasioned, and also of hearing from a Mrs. Welsh who had a strange tale to tell about her grandson Roy that was connected with Betty's appearance. Willa gave me Mrs. Welsh's phone number and suggested I might want to hear the tale for myself.

I phoned Mrs. Welsh. She was obviously surprised to hear from me after all these years. Over the phone she related the intriguing story that appears below, stressing that it is really her grandson Roy's story to tell. I expressed delight and urged her to e-mail me the text of the story. She did and I have reproduced it here.

She is most proud of her grandson Roy, who is now a high school student and a young man extraordinarily knowledgeable about the subject of ... astronomy.

From: Anita Welsh
To: John Robert Colombo
Subject: Roy's Story
Date: Tuesday, May 27, 2003 6:42 AM

Hi John:

Here is some of the story about my grandson Roy and Betty Stewart, and the so-called abduction.

There is more, but I do not want to bore you and hope it is not too long-winded.

Anita Welsh

Roy's Story

Anita Welsh

Waking with a sense that something was wrong, the realization set in that it was past 10:00 a.m.

At first, it seemed like I was waking from a bad dream. A dream I could not remember, but obviously it had such an effect that it had caused me to sleep through the alarm.

Whatever this dream had been, it had caused the whole family to sleep in. As farmers and commuters to Toronto, we were used to waking at 5:00 a.m., feeding the animals, and then getting ready to leave for our journey to work.

Stumbling half-asleep towards the kitchen, I was met by one very sleepy daughter. "Do you know what time it is?" she asked.

Nodding, I proceeded to pick up the phone to let my work, my husband's and my daughter's work know we would not be in.

As we sat down to have a cup of tea, we heard my daughter's young 2 1/2-year-old come out of his bedroom. Wiping his eyes, still half-asleep, he clambered up on the chair beside us.

"I saw God last night."

A statement like that is enough to wake anyone very quickly ... especially from one so young.

Trying not to smirk, we asked him to tell us more.

The following account not only astounded us, it lead us on a journey over the next fourteen years, one that still leaves us wondering what did happen that night.

In detail, which was amazing, as it came from a young child, was a story of how a blue light came down through his bedroom window and took him up to a space-ship.

"And how did you get through your window?" I asked. "Did God open it for you?"

A look of exasperation came over his face. "No, Nanna. I went through the glass in a blue light."

Smiling at him, I asked, "Did you not hurt yourself on the glass?"

"Nanna! I went through the glass."

A little more coaxing and he told us how, on entering the blue light, he found himself inside a room. There he met a lady, whom he described as really old, and another little boy, and a man, whom he described as God. The lady took him and the other little boy by the hand to comfort them. With "God" they walked through other rooms, where they saw what he described as animals in cages. His comment that these were not like animals on earth but were from other planets sent chills up and down our spines.

He also described meeting other little people, who looked like children, but were not. He then described them in great detail, and actually drew a picture of what they looked like. As I looked at the drawing and saw two very large black eyes staring back at me, I turned to my daughter and asked, "What have you been letting him watch on TV?"

Trying to comfort him, as he was getting angry that we did not believe him, he turned to me and said, "They told me you would not believe me. But they told me to tell you to look at page six" (I cannot now remember the correct page number) "of the book that Lennie gave you, and read the last two lines."

Puzzled, I was trying to remember… then it dawned on me. I had returned from England a few months earlier, and prior to leaving, my father had handed me a book to read on the plane. The book was strange, and I found that I could not even get past the first page, so had not bothered to even try to read more of it. On returning home, it had been thrown into the drawer of items one doesn't really want at that moment but still keep. I am sure most families have such a drawer.

As my daughter and I rummaged through the drawer, we found the book in question. As we turned to the page mentioned, we found ourselves looking at each other and then back at my grandson. The last two lines read: "There is more to heaven and earth than what any of us understand." The description was more detailed, but I remember those words standing out.

My grandson then told us that "God" would be back when he was older to see him again.

We tried to laugh it off. "Well, when he comes back, can you wake Nanna and Mummy this time, as we would like to meet him too?"

He shrugged his little shoulders. "I told you they are not coming back until I am older."

A little stunned by the last half hour, we could only make another cup of tea and try to make sense of what we had just heard. "It was a dream," I tried to convince myself.

"Maybe, Mum, but what about the book. He cannot read so how would he have known about it?" my daughter questioned.

We decided to try and forget the incident, but each night we would look up at the stars and wonder … are we in for another night of not knowing …

A few years went by, and my daughter remarried and moved away. We would occasionally tease my grandson about the incident, and he would come back with the statement, "Not yet."

Then one morning, I woke "not feeling well." Turning to my husband, I said, "Phone work, I am not going in today." With that I went back to sleep.

It was later in the morning when I woke suddenly. I did something I would never do, and that was go straight to the television and turn it on. (My first visit is to the bathroom and then to the kettle for tea — typical British.) A program was already started. A man and woman were being interviewed about an "abduction" that the woman had experienced. As I sat listening, something made me realize that this woman was the same woman who had comforted my grandson on his visit with "God." How I did not know or even why.

The urge to contact this woman was overwhelming. I phoned the television station. They informed me that this show was normally a live show, but for some reason, they had put a recording on in its place. I am not sure if the show had intended to be live, but the participants had not turned up, and this was the reason for the recording. I spoke to Mrs. McLean, the wife of the interviewer and host of the show, and told her that I had an urge to contact this woman. She told me that the woman's name was Betty and she would see if she would like to contact me.

It was only a few minutes later when the phone rang. It was Betty Stewart. We discussed in detail my grandson's so-called "visit with God." As I told her about it, she confirmed in detail exactly what my grandson had told us. She told me that she was indeed the woman that had held their hands and walked with them around the space ship. I deliberately left out some of the details of the ship, but she confirmed my worst fears — if one could call it that — that my grandson, despite his young age, had been telling the truth. She shared more details with me, details that he had also mentioned about things on the space ship.

As we were on the phone, my front door opened, and in came my daughter and grandson. We were surprised to see each other. She had decided to make a surprise visit and, of course, was shocked that I was home. Betty then asked me (when I told her that my grandson had just arrived, he was now six years old, nearly seven) to ask my grandson a few questions.

One of the questions was, "Did they feed you on the spaceship?"

My grandson startled. "They gave us a milk-like drink, but it wasn't milk." Betty then told me that, indeed, the two boys had been given a drink exactly like the one my grandson described.

Her next question seemed strange, but I asked it: "Did the little people eat with you?"

"No, Nanna, they didn't eat like us, they absorbed the food through their skin." Confused about this, I told Betty. She again confirmed that the "aliens" did not eat like humans, but did in fact eat like my grandson had said.

Although she had never met my grandson (other than during the so-called abduction), she described him in such detail that it was eerie looking at him and hearing a complete description of him.

At that moment, there was no doubt, however strange, that my grandson had met this woman. Betty then told me about a program *Man Alive* that she had been on, and said she would send me the videotape, and asked me to show it to my grandson.

A few days later the tape arrived, and I sat my grandson down to watch it. I did not tell him what it was about. As we watched, suddenly he pointed at the screen. "That is the lady on the spaceship — but her hair is funny."

I telephoned Betty and told her what my grandson had said. She laughed. "I was wearing a wig on the show — my hair is very thin and when I met your grandson, I obviously didn't have it on, as I was abducted like him during the night." This also gave sense to his original description of a very old lady. To him, at two years old, Betty would have been very old.

Over the years, Betty and I shared countless hours discussing this incident, and others that had occurred. I remember her telling me that abductions usually happen in families and generations. At this point, my back went up. "I have never been abducted!"

However, on making this remark, I remembered something that had happened to me when I was ten years old, a month either just before or just after the Queen's Coronation. In honour of the Coronation, Alexandra Palace in London was having a big fair. My parents were very strict (I had recovered from polio and rheumatic fever only a year or so before this) and they did not allow me out. That day my aunt was baby-sitting me, and she agreed to let me go to the fair with two other young girls.

What happened that day has been a mystery not only to my parents, but also to myself. According to the two young girls, I disappeared. One minute I was there, next I was gone. They thought I was hiding from them, and tried to find me, but when they couldn't, they returned home. The alarm was sounded, and a search of Alexandra Palace was made. It was not until the early hours of the morning that I was found sitting on a park bench, frightened, unable to tell anyone where I had been or with whom I had been. I could not tell anyone how I came to be sitting on the bench. My memory had been completely blocked out.

I told Betty this story and she listened thoughtfully and suggested that I had been abducted but did not remember it. She made a remark that people of our age usually had something inserted behind the ear. As she said that, my hand went instinctively to a lump just behind my right ear. This lump had appeared the night when I was ten years old. My parents had thought at first I had caught the mumps. The swelling went down, but there was always a hard lump left.

At that time, she also told me that my grandson had something inserted into his head through his nose. She also told me that children that had had this done to them were prone to nose-bleeds. Ironically, my grandson over the years has had many nose-bleeds, and despite going into hospital for them to be cauterized, he still continues to get them.

My last incident with Betty is probably even stranger. It was Christmas and I always worked on the holiday to let those with young families have the time off. This particular morning, the phone rang and a man told me that Betty had died, and her last words were that she wanted me to continue her work. I remember telling him, in no uncertain words, that I could not possibly do this. I held a very responsible position with the government and could not jeopardize my good name. Any hint of anything absurd could cause my employer to relieve me of my duties. He told me where Betty would be buried and hoped that I would reconsider.

What is so strange about this phone call is that no one could phone me direct because of my position. I went out to see my secretary to tell her that the call she had put through was to tell me of the death of a friend. Stunned, she said, "I have not put any calls through to you."

"You must have. How else could I have got the call?" I yelled back at her.

She insisted. She had been out for a coffee break and there was no one at the desk to put any calls through.

At lunch-time, when we closed and I returned home, I phoned Betty's home. I apologized to the lady who answered the phone about disturbing her on account of Betty's death, and told her that a man had phoned me earlier that morning to inform me. Her remark was even stranger. "Betty only just died — there is no man here — in fact we are just staring to let people know."

As I hung up the phone, I remembered that Betty did not know where I worked. That was one secret I kept from her. Afraid my reputation might be harmed if anyone knew of these so-called abductions, I had decided it was best that Betty never knew where or for whom I worked.

In 1997, my farm was destroyed by fire and I moved to another town. One of the things recovered from the fire, intact, was the video that Betty had sent me. All the other videos were destroyed, yet this one survived. I remember laughing as the insurance agent handed it to me.

My grandson was not ten years old when he phoned me and asked me if I would phone someone he had found a telephone number for. He wanted to talk to Terence Dickinson, one of Canada's astronomers. It seemed that my grandson after school had been going to the library to read Mr. Dickinson's books on space.

Feeling a little sheepish, I phoned Mr. Dickinson and, apologetically, told him of my grandson's request. I think he was surprised at this, but agreed to talk with him. After the call, Mr. Dickinson phoned me back and told me that he had spoken with my grandson and was astounded by Roy's knowledge of space and his books. He was surprised at the age of my grandson, and told me that most of the people who read his books were university students, studying astrophysics. He suggested that we contact a Professor Walsh at McMaster and arrange for my grandson to attend some classes there after school with other gifted students of his age group. This we did but, unfortunately, it was during the summer, and McMaster was closing. During this time, my grandson moved to British Columbia with his parents.

Not long ago, Roy, now sixteen, returned to live with me. He was going through my videotapes when he found the *Man Alive* tape and asked if he could play it. Suddenly I heard him yell, "Come here, Nan! You will never guess who was investigating Betty."

With that he rewound the tape and, to my surprise, I discovered that the person was none other than a very young Terence Dickinson.

There was no way that my grandson at ten would have known about Terence Dickinson and his connection with Betty. So now the mystery continues. What made Roy want to contact Mr. Dickinson? Is there more to this? What is the next step in this story?

From: Anita Welsh
To: John Robert Colombo
Subject: Re: Roy's Story = update
Date: Tuesday, May 27, 2003 2:05 PM

John:

I just remembered there is a footnote of interest to Roy's story. When I contacted Mrs. McLean a few weeks ago, I was trying to find a copy of the interview between yourself, Betty and Mr. McLean, her husband. Mrs. McLean remembered my call to her, despite being over 10 years ago, and told me that after that interview, they had received many calls. One of them was from the parents of another little boy who had experienced exactly the same incident as Roy that particular night. In fact they were identical tales from 2 very young children — Roy was about 2 1/2 the other little boy was about a year older I believe. But what made this astonishing is that the parents (who did not wish to be identified for fear of ridicule — exactly my reason for keeping my work secret) had taken their son to a doctor after the child was experiencing terrible nose bleeds. The doctor in surgery removed a metal type object from his nose. I understand that they were not able to identify what it was. This child was from the City of Guelph. Roy was living with me on our farm just outside of Acton, approximately 20 km from Guelph at the time of the incident. After Roy's nosebleeds starting getting worse, he was taken to Guelph to a surgeon there, who operated on him. Nothing was removed from Roy (that we know of); he still has terrible nosebleeds, so we are wondering if there is anything in there.

I do not know if Mrs. McLean has the identity of this family. I know it would have been nice to have made contact at that time, to see if the boys remembered each other.

Roy now stands 6' 2" and 280 lbs.

I would also like to add that I have now decided to get out and talk about this incident — and have approached people such as the Speaker's Bureau, in the event they should get requests for such speakers. I have also added other incidents, not related to mine, in this talk/seminar, and tried to make it light-hearted, with a little humour, yet try to analyze what lies behind all this. Although this has happened, I have tried to maintain that logically it could not have happened and there are no such beings as aliens (my former job does not help in this case); yet something lurks in the back of my mind that there has to be something — especially all the coincidences that have occurred over the years.

With this attitude, I believe I can give a talk that will appeal to both the believers and the non-believers.

If you hear of anyone wanting a seminar/talk on this type of material, I hope you will keep me in mind.

THE HOUSES ON BISHOP STREET

One day I hope to meet Lianne Gore. In the meantime we have been exchanging e-mails and accounts of ghosts on Bishop Street.

The e-mails began in a roundabout way. Ms. Gore, checking out the website of the Ghosts and Hauntings Research Society, was intrigued to learn there was an account of a ghost in a house on Bishop Street. She was curious because as a child she had lived in a house on that street — possibly in that very house.

I should explain that Bishop Street is a dead-end street off Davenport Road north of Bay Street, Toronto. It is more a laneway than it is a street. Rich in Old Country charm, it reminds me of lanes of row housing in towns in England more than it does of streets and detached dwellings characteristic of most North American towns and cities. The townhouses on both sides of Bishop Street have seen a lot of life — and death.

The haunted house described on the GHRS website was (and is) located at No. 35, but as the website does not give street numbers, Ms. Gore wanted the precise location of the haunted house. As it happens, the GHRS account was based on the one called "The Ghost on the Stairs" that appears in my book *Haunted Toronto* (1996).

It reports how two successive occupants of the two-storey town-house reported eerie experiences while living there. In the early 1980s it was the home of the beautiful opera singer Riki Turofsky, and in the late 1980s, of the talented freelance writer Andrea Reynolds. Both of these remarkable women related accounts of unusual episodes that took place there.

Now there is Lianne Gore's account. At first I thought Ms. Gore was writing about the townhouse at No. 35 Bishop Street. My jumping to conclusions led to an initial mistake. But soon that was cleared up.

The Houses on Bishop Street

Lianne Gore

Date: 24 May 2003
From: Lianne Gore
Subject: Bishop St.

Dear Mr. Colombo:

I've read your story on the Bishop St. house on GHRS that was owned by an opera singer. I would very much like to know if the house number was 41 Bishop St.

It is the last house on the dead end, on the south side of the street.

I lived in that house as a child, and believe I have an interesting story that would prove "ghostly" activities connected to that house prior to the opera singer's daughter.

Please contact me and let me know if you are interested in this story.

Sincerely,
Lianne Gore

Date: 24 May 2003
From: John Robert Colombo
Subject: Reply

Dear Ms. Gore:

Thank you for writing.

Yes, to your query about the street number of the house on Bishop St.

I would very much like to have an account of your experiences residing in the house in question, as well as of any other unusual experiences that you have had.

I will be prompt in my reply.

Sincerely,
John Robert Colombo

Date: 25 May 2003
From: Lianne Gore
Re: Bishop St.

Dear John,

I can't tell you how much it means to me to get a confirmation to my question. That house still interests me to this day because of my experience there. We moved there when I was about 7 years old, until about the age of 11. I knew we were given notice to move, as all the houses in our section of the street were to be renovated and sold. I've always had a curiosity as to just what they did with the house structure. If you like, I can draw you basic floor plans of what it looked like when I live there, and you can compare it to any information you may have.

By the way, I'm now 45 years old, so this happened many years ago....

In early December, I think it was 1967 or 1968, my mother and I had a weird experience. I was about 10 years old at the time. This happened just after midnight, on a cold snowy night. I had stayed up to help my mother sorting out things and moving furniture. Both my mother and I ended up in the hallway at the same time, after hearing a noise at the front door. (As a single-parent family, this door was locked at night.) Just as we entered the hall, my mother closer to the door than myself, the outer door opened and the street light shined into the vestibule.

My mother opened the inside glass door, and there was an old Oriental man standing there. He wore a black fedora style hat, long black overcoat, black Oriental-style pants, black Oriental slippers, and white cotton gardening style gloves. His hat and shoulders were covered with snow. My mother asked him what he wanted, and he mumbled something neither of us could understand. The entire time he was talking, he was using one hand to make chopping motions into the palm of his other hand. We kept trying to understand him, but couldn't. He was in the doorway for only 3 or 4 minutes. During the time he was in the doorway, my dog came into the hall, took one look at this old man, and went crying up the stairs with his tail tucked in.

Just as suddenly as this man showed up, he turned around and went back out the door. I went up to the doorway, and both my mother and I looked out to see where this person was going. There was no one on the street at all, and the part that really made us wonder was the fact that there wasn't one footstep in the snow. To further clarify things, the house we were living in was the last one on a dead-end street, with no exit except back up to the far end of the street.

Also in that house, my brothers and I would get yelled at for thumping on the floors, or running on the stairs … and I know many times we would all be playing quietly in one room. Many noises in that house could never be explained.

I have had other experiences in Toronto, including one who would remove my hamster from her aquarium just after moving into an apartment.

My largest/most unusual happened in Sault Ste. Marie Ont., so I'm not sure if you would be interested in reading that.

Thank you for getting back to me, I've still got the adrenalin pumping just knowing the Bishop St. house was the same one I'd lived in.

Contact me at any time, either for more information concerning this house, or any further "stories" I might be able to interest you in.

Sincerely,
Lianne Gore

Date: 26 May 2003
From: John Robert Colombo
Subject: Reply

Dear Ms. Gore:

I made a mistake. Sorry. The house that was once occupied by singer Riki Turofsky and then by writer Andrea Reynolds is located at 41 Bishop Street.

Wanting to respond right away to your e-mail, I leapt to a conclusion that this house and your house had the same address. Then I decided to check the account that appears in my book "Haunted Toronto," the basis of the material that is found on the website. Another reason that I made the connection so quickly was that my wife Ruth and I were entertained one evening (with Mr. and Mrs. Clyde Gilmour) in that very house by Riki and her partner Robert Sutner, so I have experienced its oddities first-hand. Still, the entire street has an odd "feel" to it. Seldom is one site afflicted without others sites in the immediate neighbourhood being affected. My scanner is on the fritz, but if you want to send me your mailing address or fax address, I will mail or fax to you the pages in "Haunted Toronto" devoted to the house, including photos. Despite this, I remain as interested as formerly in the account of your experiences. With your permission, I would like to work with you to develop them for possible use in a book to appear early next year.

Other experiences of yours are of interest as well. Let me know. Sorry again for jumping to conclusions!

JR

Date: 26 May 2003
From: Lianne Gore
Subject: Bishop St.

Dear Mr. Colombo,

I guess somewhere along the line our wires got crossed. In fact, the house I lived in as a child WAS 41 Bishop St. It is the last house on the south side, as you hit the end of the dead end.

There are 12 to 14 houses, all joined one to the other, and #41 is the very last one, furthest away from Davenport.

So, we very definitely ARE (unless I'm misreading this email) talking about the same house.

I would be very happy to work with you in connection with this experience, and share my other experiences with you as well.

I am very tempted to call your phone number attached to this email, but am doing my best to sit on good manners and wait to hear from you.

Lianne

She included her mailing address and telephone number (which I have deleted) so I mailed the photocopies. Once she received them, she e-mailed again.

Date: 27 May 2003
From: Lianne Gore
Subject: Bishop St.

Dear Mr. Colombo,

Thank you for mailing me your information on 35 Bishop St. That was the one house I was never in.

You couldn't get near the door for their 3 Siamese cats, and Simon was the worst. He'd attack for no reason. In one way or another, the last 6 houses on that side of the road were related.

We were in the last unit, connected to us at 39 was my godparents Joan and Mac and their 3 boys. Beside them in 37 was my godmother's sister Diane, her husband, and 3 girls. Next came the parents to Diane's husband, in 35. In 33 was the daughter to #35, Donna, her husband, son and daughter. Then in unit 31 was Donna's husband's sister, Shirley, her husband, and about 5 or 6 kids.

This probably doesn't mean anything to you, since your involvement came after-the-fact, but I thought I would share it with you.

You said you were interested in other events I've encountered, so here is one:

When I met my current husband, he was living on the first floor of 592 Woodbine Ave. Toronto, in a bachelor unit. I moved in with him

June of 1998. September 1st that same year, we moved upstairs in the same building to a one-bedroom unit.

We spent the weekend moving stuff upstairs, leaving the last few large pieces downstairs until Sunday including our hamster Rachel. Saturday night, we slept upstairs, and got back at it Sunday. We moved the last of the furniture upstairs on Sunday, and after positioning the stand for Rachel, she was the last thing moved upstairs.

When we bought Rachel, we also bought a 10 gallon rectangular glass aquarium for her home.

Sunday night, we finally had the bed in place, and slept in our bedroom for the first time. I felt like we had "company," but didn't pay any heed to it. That night, I woke up about 3 a.m. and went to the bathroom without turning on any lights. Something ran over my foot and headed to the bedroom. My first thought was that since that apartment had had rodent droppings all over, maybe this was a pet they had owned which had gotten loose and left behind. I went searching, and found it was our Rachel that was running loose. I put her back in her aquarium and went back to bed without thinking anything about it.

Monday evening, Rachel was still in the aquarium when we got home from work. That night when we went to bed, I was lying facing the door. I got a "feeling," and opened my eyes in time to see the cloudy shape of a man going down the hall away from our door. I closed my eyes again, trying to ignore it, but when I opened my eyes again, "he" was back. Every time I looked at the door, he would back away from it. Suddenly, I jumped out of bed thinking "Rachel." I went into the diningroom, and with all lights off, was feeling around in the aquarium for her. My husband woke up and came into the room, turning on the light and asked me what I was doing. I told him I was looking for Rachel, that "he" wasn't going to mess around with my pet. The aquarium was empty, and just then Rachel came out from under the bookcase and came right over to me. I put her in the aquarium, and decided to get rid of our "company."

The next day, the apartment felt "empty." I spoke with our superintendent's wife, and told her what had happened. I described to her what I saw, and she then told me that she didn't know when it happened, but supposedly a man had committed suicide in that building many years earlier.

We lived in that apartment until January 2001, and never once after that night did Rachel come out of her aquarium.

Lianne

Then came another e-mail.

Date: June 01, 2003
From: Lianne Gore
Subject: Bishop St.

Dear Mr. Colombo,

Thank you for mailing me your work on 35 Bishop St. I found it very interesting. As I said before, that was the one house in the group that I had never been in.

I must say, the story left me wondering if Carrie was still in that house, or did she leave after accomplishing her task? A follow-up would be interesting.

You had made the comment that the entire street felt weird. About 2 months ago now, my brother and I drove down that street just to "visit the old neighbourhood". I got a very eerie feeling, and just put it down to "going down memory lane" and left it at that. Who knows, I'd have to visit the street again and listen to my inner voice, but the few minutes we were there, it felt like most of the houses were watching us. It would be interesting to go back once more.

Again, thank you for sharing your work with me, and I hope to hear from you again.

Lianne Gore

As I mentioned at the beginning, I expect that one day Ms. Gore and I will meet. I expect we will meet on the sidewalk in front of the houses of Bishop Street.

GOOSEBUMPS

Sheila Greenberg is an accountant who lives and practises in Toronto.

She learned of my interest in collecting accounts of paranormal experiences, so she sent me a letter to offer to share with me and my readers an account of a prophetic dream that she had experienced many years earlier, an experience that astonishes her to this day.

I wrote back on July 9, 2003, to say, in effect: Please send the account and include as much detail as possible, adding, "I do not know how to distinguish between or among dreams, hallucinations, visions, and prophecies." Indeed, no one does.

On August 4, Mrs. Greenberg sent me her account: "I am enclosing my memory of the dream. Although it was years ago it is still very clear."

I believe that dreams like Mrs. Greenberg's occur far more often than we realize, and that most people experience them or know someone who does.

Here it is.

Goosebumps

Sheila Greenberg

This happened about forty-five years ago. My household consisted of me, husband, three sons, and a young woman, whose name was Helen. Also a cat, whose name and sex I don't remember.

Our cat was pure white and very friendly. It was allowed to roam outside, as all cats were at that time.

One day our cat disappeared, which distressed everyone. I couldn't understand it because it had been neutered. I decided that someone had scooped it. (I found out later that I was right.)

About two weeks after the disappearance, I had a dream that was so vivid I remembered every detail upon awakening.

My Dream

I awoke at the usual time and got ready to greet the day. I went into the kitchen, said hello to Helen (the only other person awake), and started to make my breakfast. Then I head a meowing at the front door. Naturally, I raced to the door, opened it, and there was our cat, safe and sound, and looking good.

Dream Over

When I woke up I was surprised that I remembered every detail of the dream. So, naturally, when I entered the kitchen, I started to relate my dream to Helen.

Believe it or not, there is meowing at the door. I open the door, and there's our cat. Everything was exactly as in my dream.

I have goosebumps on my arms and legs as I write this!

A MOST SPECTACULAR SIGHT

Lucie Romanycia is an excellent observer and investigator. She is also a fine correspondent, so it is a simple matter for the reader of the letter that she sent to me to visualize the sight in the night sky that she and other members of her family saw from the patio of the family home in St. Louis, Saskatchewan. The letter also conveys a sense of excitement at the "spectacular sight," a sighting that lasted only four or five minutes but will remain with her for the rest of her life.

Accompanying the letter was the correspondent's sketch of what she saw in the sky drawn in four colours: cadmium red, light pink, light blue, and dark blue. The left-hand side of the disk, ball, or sphere appears in red with some purple highlighting, whereas the object's right-hand side appears in blue with some purple highlighting as well. The UFO emits red, blue, and white sparks, a most wondrous sight to behold!

It is difficult to know what to make of the object or image. It was moving too slowly to be an airplane. Perhaps it was a helicopter, but it seems unlikely that there are helicopters with bright, multi-coloured search lights. Could it be connected with the Northern Lights? Maybe it was an alien spacecraft. It is possible — indeed, likely — that we will never know the real cause of the "spectacular sight." In the meantime, we should be grateful to Mrs. Romanycia for taking pains to recall what she and her three sisters saw that night and then deciding to share it with us.

A Most Spectacular Sight

Lucie Romanycia

August 19, 2000

Dear Mr. Colombo:

It was good talking to you last night and to know that you are still interested in supernatural experiences.

The first time that I wrote to you, on Sept. 6, 1990, I mentioned that eight people witnessed a UFO on June 29, 1974. This time four of us witnessed a UFO on July 31, 2000.

On Monday, July 31, 2000, at approximately 11:25 p.m., I was sitting outside on the patio gazing east at a dark sky. All of a sudden my eyes saw a most spectacular sight. Shaped like a volleyball, it was the most beautiful display of red and blue bright sparkling lights that shone like gems with rays darting out like shooting stars. It was travelling from east to west, at a speed of about 15-20 miles an hour. The bright pulsating ball was approximately 400-500 feet from the house and at approximately 80-90 feet in the air. It shone so brightly that it left me mesmerized. A sight to behold like you should expect to see upon entering Ali Baba's cave. Only this was not in a cave but red and blue sparkling jewels in a dark sky.

The patio door was open so I called my oldest sister Blandine who was finishing her lunch in the adjoining kitchen. I told her to hurry if she wanted to see something beautiful sparkling in the sky. My sister immediately came out. The two of us admired the bright coloured object. On the outside left of the ball, the cadmium red was darker in colour. On the outside right the sparkling blue was darker in colour. Lighter red and lighter sky blue almost like diamonds glowing in the middle. The blue side of the ball was pulsating a bit more than the red side. I do not know if the muffled purring sound came from the UFO or from the noise caused by cars on the No. 2 Highway.

Knowing that my two other sisters, Monique and Colombe, would enjoy looking at this bright coloured phenomenon, I ran upstairs to get them. They both followed me outside. Behind the pines and the maples only the bright red sparkles could be seen. The object had now become smaller as it sailed away towards the south-west. The four of us watched until the ball finally disappeared in the dark behind the trees. The spectacular sight lasted for approximately 4-5 minutes.

Aftermath

On August 1, at 7:50 a.m., I phoned 306-763-7421 — CKBI radio station in Prince Albert. This city is approximately 30 km from St. Louis. I explained everything to Mr. Wade Custer after I had asked him if anyone had reported a UFO sighting. No reports had come in so Wade said that he would call me back after he'd made a phone call. Mr. Custer phoned at approximately 9:04 a.m. and told me that he had contacted the airport. The personnel there had no knowledge of planes or helicopters flying the night of July 31. They did not know what the object could be. "Who should I call?" I asked. Wade suggested that I contact the Saskatoon weather bureau. At approximately 9:15 a.m. I phoned 306-975-6906 and explained once again about the spectacular sight to Don Ryback. He could not help as he had no knowledge as to the identity of this round sparkling object. Mr. Ryback advised me to call the RCMP. I did call 306-233-5810 at approximately 9:30 a.m., got Regina headquarters twice instead of the Wakaw detachment. A lady at the Regina office listened to my story. She found it mighty interesting so she helped me connect with the RCMP in Wakaw. I left a message at the Wakaw Depot to call me. Sergeant Scarf called me at approximately 12:50 p.m. He thought that I had an interesting story. He said that an officer from Wakaw had been in St. Louis on July 31, at about the same time that my sisters and I had spotted the UFO but this officer hadn't reported anything about a sighting. To this statement I answered, "The officer who was in St. Louis would have probably been in his car with his eyes on the road — not looking at the sky like I was." Sergeant Scarf retorted, "Oh well, that's right!"

On this same day, at approximately 2:20 p.m., I saw an army plane flying south to north on the west side of the house. Whether this had any connections to the sighting, I do not know.

Lucie Romanycia

OTHER BOOKS ON THE MYSTERIOUS
by John Robert Colombo

SURVEYS

Colombo's Book of Marvels (1979)
Mysterious Canada (1988, 1998)
The Little Blue Book of UFOs (1992)
Ghost Stories of Ontario (1995)
Haunted Toronto (1996)
Mysteries of Ontario (1999)
Three Mysteries of Nova Scotia (1999)
The UFO Quote Book (1999)
Ghost Stories of Canada (2000)
True Canadian Ghost Stories (2003)

PERSONAL ACCOUNTS SERIES

Extraordinary Experiences (1989)
Mysterious Encounters (1990)
Mackenzie King's Ghost (1991)
UFOs over Canada (1991)
Dark Visions (1992)
Close Encounters of the Canadian Kind (1994)
Ghosts Galore! (1994)
Closer than You Think (1998)

STORIES SERIES

Strange Stories (1994)
Marvellous Stories (1998)
Singular Stories (1999)
Ghosts in Our Past (1999)
Weird Stories (2000)
Many Mysteries (2001)

MONOGRAPH SERIES

Conjuring Up the Owens (1999)
Lambert's Day (1999)
The Occult Webb (1999)
O Rare Denis Saurat (2003)

AN INVITATION

If you have an odd or eerie experience that you are willing to share with me and with the readers of my books, why not contact me? Send me an e-mail at *jrc@ca.inter.net* or write to me:

> John Robert Colombo
> c/o Editorial Department
> The Dundurn Group
> 8 Market Street, Suite 200
> Toronto, ON, Canada
> M5E 1M6

Visit my website at *www.colombo.ca*.